Margie,

Your support through the years have been a sound foundation for me. Your passion and good sense have been a challenge I have tried to embrace. I hope you find joy and hope in this book. May God continue to bless and keep you.

Love,
Bob

Divine Providence

God's Program for Humankind

Robert A. Gunderson

Eloquent Books
New York, New York

Copyright © 2009 Robert A. Gunderson.
All rights reserved.
No part of this book may be reproduced or transmitted in any form or by any means, graphic, electronic, or mechanical, including photocopying, recording, typing, or by any information storage retrieval system, without the permission in writing from the publisher.

Eloquent Books
An imprint of AEG Publishing Group
845 Third Avenue, 6th Floor—6016
New York, NY 10022
http://www.eloquentbooks.com

ISBN: 978-1-60860-614-6

Book Design: Bruce Salender

Printed in the United States of America.

dedicated to my mother,
Dorothy Etzenhouser Gunderson

teacher, nurturer, disciple

Contents

Foreword	7
Introduction	11
The Nature of the Divine	20
The Creation Myths	30
A New Creation Myth	37
The Natural World	58
The Triune God	80
The Human Condition	96
Revelation and Inspiration	104
Sin and Salvation	114
Divine Providence	132
Meaning and Purpose in Mortal Life	150
The Church	159
From Believer to Disciple	170

Foreword

The modern world presents a daunting face to those of us who try to be aware of what is going on. The marvels of technology allow us a daily glimpse into events and conditions around the globe. We are bombarded on all sides with news of catastrophes already in progress and trends which appear to be leading toward greater disasters in a wide range of human endeavors. Yet in the midst of great troubles we also find the best qualities of humankind being exemplified. Many people are spending themselves to resolve conflicts, alleviate suffering, assert positive change, and right wrongs. Whether acting from common humanity, political conviction, or religious belief, such people give expression to one of the basic tenets of all the world's major faiths: we are our brother's keepers; we do have responsibility for the well-being of our fellow humans. While we may be encouraged by the activity of so many to address human challenges, we are also struck by the apparent lack of coordination in such efforts. This situation is a reflection and a characteristic of what has become known as post-modernism.

Post-modernism is the assertion that there is not, nor can there be, one universal truth for humankind, nor can the human mind comprehend the truth that does exist. Such a view is a negation of the primary stance of the previous age, modernism, which asserted that the natural world is ordered, humankind can discover that order, and by discovering the order of the universe humankind can control it for our benefit.[1] Modernism created the current Western world and is the paradigm by which it continues to function day-to-day. The problem is that many people no longer believe the premises on which modernism is based and therefore find themselves adrift to create their own value system by which to steer. The traditional religions which once provided such basic orientation for their civilizations have lost credibility in the face of the scientific paradigm because they have failed to reframe their fundamental concepts in terms that fully appreciate and incorporate the current human situation and condition. Such a reframing for Christianity is the purpose of this book.

A fundamental premise of every major religion is the unity and ultimacy of the Divine, which it seeks to honor and follow. The Divine is held to be the one and only First Cause or Creator of all that exists. Yet the theology and practice of each faith, each developed within a particular culture, tend to present the Divine as focused on and relevant only to those who respond to its particular revelation or insight. People outside that faith due to geography, time, or choice, are held to be excluded from the full favor and blessing of the Divine. Each religion requires people to come under the influence of its particular belief system and accept its truth to benefit and receive the blessing of its Divine promise. Such an attitude limits the Divine and contradicts the religion's assertion of the basic comprehensiveness of the divine nature.

Through the ages, some in each religion have asserted a less restricted and dogmatic view of the religion's insights. The mystics and spiritualists of each faith tradition have tried to express a more universal and inclusive vision. But the visions these mystics attempt to describe are of a realm beyond the ordinary world and outside of the experience and comprehension of the majority of people. While often respected and honored, the mystical tradi-

---

[1] See Huston Smith, *Beyond the Post-Modern Mind* (Wheaton, Illinois: Quest Books, 1982), 3-16 for a clear and concise discussion of this subject.

Foreword

tions of the major faiths have been marginalized by the spiritual and administrative leadership as impractical or inaccessible for most believers. Some efforts have been made to distill a synthesis of the mystical traditions of the various faiths that emphasizes their commonality for humankind. In the West, this has come to be known as the perennial philosophy.

While the perennial philosophy has been a common ground for seekers, mystics, and theologians of all religious traditions for centuries, disciples of each particular faith tend to find it nebulous, a bit foreign, and somewhat academic because of its inclusiveness and generality. A few modern scholars have attempted to explore the world's religions with a view to improving cross-cultural understanding and appreciation of each faith by open-minded people. The work of Huston Smith in the United States of America and Frithjof Schuon in Europe are exemplary. But both have tended to adopt, at least tacitly, the postmodern paradigm that allows for multiple versions of Truth, without providing guidance to individual religious practitioners. If there is more than one true religion, how can the truth of *my* religion be ultimate and command my total allegiance? What is needed is the development of the principles of the philosophy within each of the enduring religions that work through the exclusive limitations imposed by the respective theologies accumulated over time.

The technologically-driven shrinking of the earth and the increasing interspersion of peoples and cultures make tolerance of and appreciation of different religious beliefs and practices essential for any hope of peace and cooperation within humankind. This book is an attempt to provide a new, expanded look at the perennial philosophy through the lens of Christianity. References to other faith traditions are not judgments of these faiths but are intended to place Christianity in the context of our modern multicultural world. It is for devotees and scholars of the other faith traditions to develop similar works for their faiths.

This book is not a scholarly work; it makes no effort to exhaustively mine the production of previous thinkers and build up a body of evidence in support of a point of view. Rather, it is

Divine Providence: God's Program for Humankind

more of an essay that draws on a body of ancient and modern wisdom, and on the work of scholars and other published sources in a variety of fields to address problems and issues dividing people from each other. I claim no originality, but have gleaned my thoughts from a lifetime of study and contemplation. I have acknowledged specific sources wherever I can identify them.

Introduction

The world is too much with us; late and soon,
Getting and spending, we lay waste our powers:
Little we see in nature that is ours;
We have given our hearts away, a sordid boon![2]
—William Wordsworth

The Christian theological concept of providence has fallen out of favor in recent years and is seldom the subject of contemporary preaching and teaching in the church. I suspect this is due largely to the inadequacy of many versions of providence in light of the Enlightenment and the intellectual debunking of myth in general that has characterized the developments of the modern Western world. Providence is God's plan for humankind. Even the idea that God has a plan for humankind is no longer accepted by many. Modern people insist, as some have always done, that the truth to which they commit themselves must be consistent with their senses, perceptions, and experiences. But many people everywhere and in every time have rec-

---

[2] William Wordsworth, "The World Is too Much With Us," *A Treasury of the World's Best Loved Poems* (New York: Avenel Books, 1961), 47–48.

Divine Providence: God's Plan for Humankind

ognized that the natural world, including humankind, exists and functions in ways that exceed our understanding and control. Religion in its various forms grows out of people's deeply felt need to try to make sense of and relate to the world in which we find ourselves. Something greater than ourselves is at work.

In the pre-modern world, people universally identified the greater something responsible for the natural world as a Divine Force or Being or group of Beings. Their attempts to relate to the Divine created religion.[3] With the Enlightenment and the rise of science, many Western people embraced science and technology as a substitute for religion. The assertion was that humankind can indeed discover how the world works and learn to control it for their benefit. But people have increasingly found that this paradigm is also failing in its promise, as further developments in science raise greater doubts as to our ever discovering the fundamental nature of the natural world. The technology we have developed to serve humankind threatens to destroy not only our civilizations but much of the natural world as well. Moreover, science and technology provide no moral guidance or sense of purpose and meaning for our existence. This disillusionment with modernity has created what is termed post-modernity.

Post-modernity is not a new worldview or universal paradigm, but rather the belief, or at least the suspicion, that there is no universal paradigm by which humankind can steer with confidence. Post-modern people increasingly admit to feeling what Jean-Paul Sartre has called the God-shaped hole in human consciousness, where the divine has always been but has been driven out by modernity.[4] People increasingly want what religion has traditionally provided but many are unable or unwilling to go back to the discredited concepts of pre-modern theology. New religious understandings that account for and embrace advances and developments of science, humanities, and cultures of the present-day world are desperately needed.

---

[3] See Huston Smith, *Forgotten Truth* (New York: HarperSanFrancisco, 1976), v–x.
[4] Armstrong, *The Battle for God* (New York: Ballantine Books, 2000), 199.

Introduction

Religions come in a wide variety of shapes and sizes depending on the quality of the vision which impels them. The world's great and enduring religions have spoken profoundly to the societies in which they emerged and have been defining paradigms in shaping major civilizations. They have provided a vision of how humankind fits into the created world and relates to the Divine. In general terms, the great Eastern religions—Hinduism, Buddhism, and Taoism—have presented the Divine as the creative and organizing force or set of principles that human beings are to discover and to which we are to conform. The great Western religions—Judaism, Christianity, and Islam—have posited a Deity, also creative and organizing, but with aspects of personality to whom humans are to relate in accordance with parameters established by the Deity. The parameters the religion believes to have been established by the Deity for human conduct, the activity of the Deity relative to humankind, and the results of such activity and conduct are known as divine providence. At their core, all major religions have provided relevant concepts for human behavior, but the accumulation of ritual practices, moral standards, exclusionary judgments, and structures of authority need to be recast to reflect modern civilizational practices and identities to keep them relevant for their adherents.

Modern Western society is unique in the history of humankind in its development of a largely secular paradigm for understanding and dealing with the world based on science rather than religion.[5] In terms of understanding how the natural world works and in providing a basis for technology that allows us a measure of control over our environment, at least in the short term, science has proven powerful indeed. But science and technology are unable to provide answers to the most fundamental questions of human values and the meaning and purpose of life. Science cannot tell us *why* we exist, how we *should* spend our lives, and *what happens* to us when we die. For many people religion still fills that role. But the rise of science has dealt a crippling blow

---

[5] See Smith, *Forgotten Truth,* for a concise discussion of this phenomena.

Divine Providence: God's Plan for Humankind

to the manner in which religion has traditionally explained meaning and purpose, because the myths and symbols by which religion expressed its values had, over time, come to be mistakenly understood as literal, actual, and historical by most people, including many religious leaders. Because science is so successful in exploring the nature of the natural world, many theologians, philosophers, and metaphysicians have tried to adopt the methods of science rather than drawing the necessary distinctions between the material and the spiritual/metaphysical worlds.[6] Instead of seeking myths and symbols suitable for modern people, these theologians, philosophers, and metaphysicians have deconstructed the old myths and left modern people stranded in a world they can not understand and from which they feel increasingly alienated.[7]

A few modern thinkers have worked at reframing the myths and symbols of religion to provide a meaningful way of seeing the modern world,[8] but most Western religious leaders have focused their efforts on accommodating religion to the paradigm of modern science.[9] Modernity, which is based on the Newtonian model of the physical world and the Darwinian hypothesis

---

[6] World Religions expert Huston Smith has written a series of books dealing with this situation. These include *Forgotten Truth, The Common Vision of the World's Religions* (New York: HarperSanFrancisco, 1976); *Beyond the Post-Modern Mind* (Wheaton, Illinois: The Theosophical Publishing House, 1982); and *Why Religion Matters* (New York: HarperSanFrancisco, 2001).

[7] See Armstrong, *The Battle for God,* xv–xviii for a cogent and astute analysis of this phenomenon.

[8] In addition to Huston Smith's work cited above, I have been particularly impressed by the work of Frithjof Schuon in developing modern understandings of the foundational myths and symbols of all the major world religions. See, for example, his books *Understanding Islam*, (Bloomington, Indiana: World Wisdom Books, Inc., 1994); *In the Tracks of Buddhism*, Sydney, Australia: Allen and Unwin, 1968); *The Transfiguration of Man* (Bloomington, Indiana: World Wisdom Books, Inc., 1995); and *The Transcendent Unity of Religions* (Wheaton, Illinois, The Theosophical Publishing House, 1984).

[9] See Van A. Harvey, *The Historian and the Believer* (Champaign, Illinois: University of Illinois Press, 1966), for several illustrations of efforts by modern theologians and philosophers to accommodate religion to the pervasive paradigm of science.

of the natural world, asserts that humanity holds its destiny in its own hands, subject only to the chance operation of the natural, unconscious but lawful forces by which it was shaped. Progress toward a universal utopia is seen as both our hope and inevitable destiny.

But that destiny has only to do with this world. Modernity either denies the reality of non-material worlds or simply ignores such considerations because science has no way of investigating and controlling them. Accordingly, within mainstream Western cultures, religion has too often become a way for people to cope with an unperfected and largely impersonal, deterministic world because we have no way of discovering its meaning and purpose. Values have become existential, humanistic, and situational rather than universal, divinely instituted, and eternal. More fundamentalist denominations and traditions have tended to hold a dualistic understanding of the world; their view seems to be that this world is essentially evil, under the temporary control of demonic forces. Ultimately God will defeat these demonic forces in a terribly destructive confrontation and usher in an era of righteousness, peace, and prosperity. Those who align themselves with God according to the tenets of fundamentalism can both prosper now and enjoy the protection and triumph of God in the coming apocalypse. The fundamentalist view tends to discount the validity of the scientific paradigm, not because it is flawed, but because it is demonic.[10] Such views cause dissension and conflict between people within the same society and result in political, social, and intellectual competition that is becoming increasingly disruptive and destabilizing. In the extreme, fundamentalist "conservative" groups are adopting increasingly militant reactions against their more liberal "progressive" neighbors.

On the other hand there are people who attempt to bring religion into the human sphere by making the Divine an extension of the human mind and spirit. For them, that which science cannot explain or control is unreal, a deception played on the gullible by charlatans, or the wishful thinking of the uneducated and

---

[10] See Armstrong, *The Battle for God*.

superstitious. Humanistic religious systems have been espoused which bring God into the material world with limited power, able only to react to the development of history driven by human actions and random natural forces.

In the face of terrible destructive forces unleashed by the science of desperate, ambitious, and/or immoral leaders in the twentieth century, many people today have concluded that the promises of modernity have failed. Instead of the constant progress toward utopia that was envisioned, the world has suffered greater crises, and serious and pervasive deterioration of the both the physical and moral environments are evident. Moreover, in science itself the ordered and definitive world of Newtonian physics has given way to quantum mechanics and its counter-intuitive phenomena. Instead of steadily unraveling the mysteries of the material world, scientists have continued to expose more vistas of unimaginable wonder that bring into question much that we thought we understood.[11] Those who feel the modern worldview has been deconstructed find themselves not with a new worldview, but with no worldview. They feel there can be no over-arching paradigm by which to understand either the natural world or the human situation. For them, purpose is situational and meaning existential. In practical day-to-day terms, postmodern people still function under the modern paradigm; it just does not provide them with any long-term or ultimate hope.

In a recent book, political scientist Samuel P. Huntington has compellingly described the manner in which humanity currently seems to be orienting itself.[12] In the post-Cold War era, Huntington sees humankind globally dividing itself into a small number of great civilizations based on, or at least identified definitively by, the great world religions. While not all of the people comprising these civilizations are themselves religious, they use religion and the values and traditions these have come to represent to differentiate themselves from other civilizations. Competition

---

[11] See Smith, *Beyond the Post-Modern Mind*, 1–16.
[12] Samuel P. Huntington, *The Clash of Civilizations and the Remaking of World Order* (New York: Simon & Schuster, 1996).

Introduction

between these civilizations encompasses all aspects of life: religious, political, economic, military, and social. While the vast majority of people throughout the world remain primarily oriented by local conditions and the traditions of their immediate society, political, military and economic leaders and the controllers of nations everywhere have been exposed to the modern Western paradigm and largely interact with each other on that basis. The decisions that create worldwide developments are made largely on the basis of the perceived best interest of these leaders and their constituents, those who keep them in positions of power and influence. Once again, and more pervasively than ever before, religions are being pressed into the service of humanist and secular values and goals. Religions, seen and used in this manner, provide competing views of the divine intention for humankind. Both the nature of the Divine and the manner in which it relates to human beings are presented in ways that appear mutually exclusive between each particular religion and their civilizations. The gods, however perceived, seem each to require compliance with their particular scheme in order for humankind to realize the truth and the fulfillment of their created nature.

Certainly fundamentalists, an increasingly vocal and politically active group in several of the world's religions, understand the imperatives of their religion in these terms. The survival of each religion and its civilization seems, ultimately, to depend on the conversion—or at least submission—of all others to their version of Truth. As most often perceived, this earth and its inhabitants are in a zero-sum game with finite resources; the success of one group necessarily means the failure of other groups. Increasingly, fundamentalists in each civilization see their most cherished values under attack, and the extremists in each society are adopting increasing militant stances vis-à-vis their perceived opponents and oppressors.

Secularists within each civilization tend to disassociate themselves from the religious focus of their fundamentalist neighbors and try to frame the competition between their civilization and others in political and economic terms. However, to

Divine Providence: God's Plan for Humankind

win wide support for their particular ideology, they either must develop their political and/or economic system as a substitute religion or frame it in quasi-religious terms. This is because religion enlists spiritual and emotional aspects as well as the mental and physical, while politics and economics do not. The humanist values of the educated minority do not have wide appeal to the masses. "People have a profound need to believe that the truth they perceive is rooted in the unchanging depths of the universe; for were it not, could the truth be really important?"[13] Communism tried to debunk traditional religion and put humanistic values in its place, but this ideology failed fundamentally both because their leaders continued to change the values to suit themselves and because the common people could not relate to the current party line and find personal fulfillment in its cold, mechanistic materialism. They found themselves being exploited without hope.

Capitalism and democracy as practiced in the West have long been yoked with Christianity, though unevenly and often grudgingly and even cynically. The hope it offers to individuals and to oppressed minorities is that by hard work, cleverness, and a bit of luck individuals and groups might prosper. This has served as a pressure-relief valve for Western civilization throughout the rise of modernity. But the inherent contradiction between the self-serving values of capitalism and the self-abasing ideal of Christianity exposes the partnership to charges of hypocrisy, the bane of even the humanistic values of modernity. The erosion of confidence in modernity within Christian civilization and the globalization of capitalism, with its growing interdependence with non-Western civilizations, have fostered post-modernism and exposed the mis-identification of capitalism's Christian roots.

Every age and society has had its share of challenges, and each has had its share of doomsayers. While this assessment of the current human situation is dark indeed, there is still hope to be found in traditional religion. But it requires a reframing of the

---

[13] Smith, *Forgotten Truth*, v.

Introduction

manner in which religions understand and express the myths and theologies they employ for relating the human to the Divine. Forty years ago Professor John Macquarrie identified five Christian doctrines that must be addressed in this increasing secular age if the religion is to speak with clarity and authority to modern Western people.[14] These doctrines are (1) creation, (2) incarnation, (3) church, (4) sacramental presence, and (5) eschatology. These will each be addressed in this exploration of the concept of divine providence. We begin with some reflection on the nature of the Divine.

---

[14] John Macquarrie, *New Directions in Theology Today, (Volume III, God and Secularity)* (Philadelphia: Westminster Press, 1967), 128–138.

The Nature of the Divine

God is a sphere whose center is everywhere and whose circumference is nowhere. [15]

—St. Bonaventure

Every major religion is founded on a vision of the Divine. Whether that vision came from revelatory experiences, deep contemplation, dialogue between scholars with their cumulative inspiration over centuries, or some combination of them all, the authority and efficacy of a religion depends on its ability to communicate to masses of people some understanding of the nature and purpose of the Divine. The basic sacred texts of Hinduism were created by unidentified mystics in undocumented times. How their profound insights into the divine nature were discovered/revealed will probably never be known. Additional texts were added over the centuries from the experiences and contemplations of disciples devoted to the quest for enlightenment. Buddhism began from the spiritual struggles and contemplative persistence of one individual who "pierced the veil" and

---

[15] Quoted in Philip Novak, *The World's Wisdom* (New York: HarperSanFrancisco, 1994), 269.

The Nature of the Divine

then spent his life attempting to share his understandings with all who would listen. Though he himself probably never wrote down his insights into the divine nature, his teachings were recorded by disciples and preserved, with many amendments, interpretations, and additions, for modern people. Confucianism grew out of the practical work of one man to apply insights gleaned from the classical writings of earlier poets and thinkers to the governance of society. He did not think of his work as religious and offered no insights into any transcendent realm. But his teachings assumed a transcendent order of things and his followers gradually formalized the vision of a hierarchical structure that tied the fate of the mundane world to the spiritual realm of the ancestors going all the way back to the first ancestors of the Chinese people. Confucianism has little appeal outside Chinese culture, but some of its insights into social, ethical, and political behavior have universal application. Taoism is said to have developed from the insight of a legendary mystic who reluctantly distilled ancient wisdom into a brief and enigmatic document prior to riding off into obscurity. The origins of this wisdom are equally obscure to us, but again, followers have interpreted and amplified the teachings and practices over the centuries.

Western religions resulted from more direct divine intervention in human affairs. Judaism cites the divine callings of Noah, Abraham, and Moses, and their subsequent covenants with the Divine, as its basis. These historical events are held to have been initiated by God. Through the Hebrew prophets, God continued to reveal both himself and his intentions for his covenant people. Christianity makes the boldest claim of all major religions: God became human in the person of Jesus of Nazareth. The record of what Jesus said and did is the disclosure in human terms of both the nature of the Divine and the divine will for humankind. Christians believe that God is always active in this world in the form of the Holy Spirit and that Jesus, as a resurrected and glorified being, will return to this world to effect its culmination. Islam arose from the transmission of God's program for humanity by the angel Gabriel to the Prophet Mohammad. The Qur'an in Arabic is held by Muslims to be the actual words of God and

Divine Providence: God's Plan for Humankind

final authority for God's intentions for humankind. The writings of all the major faiths provide insight into what believers understand to be the nature, purpose, and activity of the Divine from the human perspective.

All major religions assert that the Divine in its essential nature is transcendent. In the words of the Taoist teaching,

> "The Tao [Divine] that can be told is not the eternal Tao.
> The name that can be named is not the eternal name.
> The nameless is the beginning of heaven and earth.
> The named is the mother of ten thousand things [symbols or manifestations].
> Ever desireless, [free of ego] one can see the mystery.
> Ever desiring, [self-aware] one can see the manifestations.
> These two spring from the same source but differ in name; this appears as darkness.
> Darkness within darkness.
> The gate to all mystery."
>
> —Tao Te Ching - One.[16]

In their most profound understandings, all major religions assert that the reality of the Divine cannot be comprehended by the human mind; it must be experienced by the essence of the human, the spirit or soul or whatever term the religion uses for the part of each human being that is eternal. Yet paradoxically they also assert that in specific ways the Divine makes itself known in our conscious awareness and calls all people into relationship with it. In every case, religions finally must be framed in human, this-worldly terms for us to be able to deal with the Divine at all. Whether the aim of the religion is to free us from the illusionary nature of the material world or to effect the ultimate transformation of this finite and transitory world into the eternal kingdom of God, religions try to take us from where and

---

[16] Quoted in *The Ways of Religion*, Roger Eastman, ed. (New York: Harper & Row, 1975), 253.

The Nature of the Divine

what we are to wherever and whatever the Divine is and intends us to be.

The nature of transcendence is the topic of mystics and spiritual revealers in all the major religious traditions. But because the transcendent is utterly different from the material world, those who try to give expression about it are at a loss to formulate and communicate meaningful concepts. This difficulty was addressed by the Christian mystic Saint John of the Cross (1542–1591):

> "We receive this mystical knowledge of God clothed in none of the kinds of images, in none of the sensible representations, which our mind makes use of in other circumstances. Accordingly in this knowledge, since the senses and the imagination are not employed, we get neither form nor impression, nor can we give any account or furnish any likeness, although the mysterious and sweet-tasting wisdom comes home so clearly to the inmost part of our soul. Fancy a man seeing a certain kind of thing for the first time in his life. He can understand it, use and enjoy it, but he cannot apply a name to it, nor communicate any idea of it, even though all the while it be a mere thing of sense. How much greater will be his powerlessness when it goes beyond the senses! This is the peculiarity of the divine language. The more infused, intimate, spiritual and supersensible it is, the more does it exceed the senses, both inner and outer, and impose silence upon them....The soul then feels as if placed in a vast and profound solitude, to which no created thing has access, in an immense and boundless desert, desert the more delicious the more solitary it is. There in this abyss of wisdom, the soul grows by what it drinks in from the well-springs of the comprehension of love,...and recognizes, however sublime and learned may be the terms we employ, how utterly

vile, insignificant, and improper they are, when we seek to discourse of divine things by their means."[17]

Swedish theologian and mystic Emanuel Swedenborg (1688–1772) wrote numerous books based on his repeated experiences in the spiritual world. He characterized the Divine as a spiritual sun emanating divine love and wisdom, as our physical sun emanates warmth and light, but he was careful to affirm that the spiritual world was not a place, but rather was a condition. Time, space, and physical life as we experience them have no counterpart in the spiritual world. Rather the spiritual world is based on *quality* rather than *quantity*. But since we humans can not conceive of existence without regard to time and space, he was forced to use physical analogies to attempt to share his experiences.[18]

Another characteristic of the works of the mystics is their effort to express the otherness of the Divine relative to the human. Yet, paradoxically, the experience of the Divine is one in which the individual feels completely at home, secure, blissful, cherished, and at peace. Many seekers of the Divine describe the *journey* toward this otherness as harrowing, dreadful, and terribly demanding, requiring an almost complete deconstruction of all ties to the natural world. Every faith provides sets of instructions—spiritual disciplines—to guide those who would embark on such a course. In every major faith tradition there are those who dedicate their lives to such disciplines. They report mixed results: some claim breakthroughs of enlightenment, while others seem to languish for years in frustration and dimness.

Yet to some individuals, the sense of the Divine comes almost unbidden. Sarah Pierrepoint Edwards, the wife of the early American theologian and preacher Jonathan Edwards (1703 – 1758), related her experience:

---

[17] Saint John of the Cross, *The Dark Night of the Soul*, book ii, ch. Xvii. Quoted in William James, *The Varieties of Religious Experience* (New York: Mentor Books, 1958), 312-313.

[18] See Emanuel Swedenborg, *Divine Love and Wisdom* (West Chester, Pennsylvania: Swedenborg Foundation, 2003).

The Nature of the Divine

"Last night was the sweetest night I ever had in my life.... Part of the night I lay awake, sometimes asleep, and sometimes between sleeping and waking. But all night I continued in a constant, clear, and lively sense of the heavenly sweetness of Christ's excellent love, of his nearness to me, and of my dearness to him; with an inexpressibly sweet calmness of soul in an entire rest in him. I seemed to myself to perceive a glow of divine love come down from the heart of Christ in heaven into my heart in a constant stream, like a stream or pencil of sweet light. At the same time my heart and soul all flowed out in love to Christ, so that there seemed to be a constant flowing and reflowing of heavenly love, and I appeared to myself to float or swim, in these bright, sweet beams, like the motes swimming in the beams of the sun, or the streams of his light which come in at the window. I think that what I felt each minute was worth more than all the outward comfort and pleasure which I had enjoyed my whole life put together. It was pleasure, without the least sting, or any interruption. It was sweetness, which my soul was lost in; it seemed to be all that my feeble frame could sustain."[19]

Mrs. Edwards' account reflects her Christian frame of reference; such experience always has a cultural context. But her account also contains elements common to the experiences of persons from all mystical traditions: the sense of complete acceptance by the Divine, the sense that the reality of the Divine is of a different and vastly superior order than the mundane world, and yet the sense of being completely at home and at peace in this presence.

In every major religion the Divine is manifest in the natural world in a form or multiple forms designed to *symbolize* its transcendent reality and serve as a focus and bridge or pathway to that reality. Such manifestations are always appropriate to the

---

[19] Quoted in James, *Varieties of Religious Experience*, 219–220.

culture into which they are introduced. Understood within the context which it serves, each manifestation is true, but seen from the perspective of other cultural contexts, the manifestation appears to be a false representation of the Divine. Furthermore, cultural contexts and manifestations are time-specific; as cultures develop or change over time, the symbols must also develop and be re-interpreted to remain authentic. Thus, our concept of the Divine requires an appreciation of the context of its manifestation in every successive generation and every re-mixing of cultural composition. Traditional religions, while showing great resilience overall, struggle within themselves with this process.

Of the major issues facing humanity as we strive to comprehend the Divine, two related issues stand out: anthropomorphism, the ascribing of human characteristics to Deity; and the limitations of human language. For there to be a relationship between human and Divine, it is required that the manifestation(s) of the Divine take a form appropriate to the natural world. In many primitive religions the elements of the natural world assume spiritual dimensions, with heavenly bodies, geological features, animals, trees, or weather phenomena becoming identified with spirits. Religious practices in such religions involve rituals addressed to these forces or entities in hopes of establishing a favorable relationship with them. Many early civilizations developed concepts of the earth as divine mother, the source of life, and the sun as divine father, the giver of light, warmth, and power. Various personifications of rain, wind, the sea, mountains, and rivers were developed to help people deal with otherwise uncontrollable and often hostile factors affecting human life. This tendency to personify natural forces and identify them with the Divine attests to humanity's assessment that persons are the highest form of being in the natural world.[20] All of the manifestations of the Divine in the major religions have forms or as-

---

[20] While it may be true that "the God of horses has four legs," the existence of the Divine is not dependent on its anthropomorphism; it is not just a projection of human wishful thinking. Humans sense deity long before they give it human form.

The Nature of the Divine

pects that are personal in character; even in tribal religions that use animal forms to embody spiritual beings, the animals have human or super-human traits such as the ability to speak, to reason, or to feel emotions.

Anthropomorphism, when properly understood, makes possible the development of personal relationship between the human and Divine. But it becomes a problem in religion when people lose sight of the symbolic nature of divine manifestations. When they are treated as literal or are worshipped in themselves, they become idols and false gods incapable of developing the spiritual nature within each to a maturity in which the true nature of the Divine can be appreciated. When the symbol becomes the reality, it loses its ability to function properly and spiritual development is truncated. Inevitably, such manifestations become made in our natural image rather than calling us to develop into the spiritual image of the Divine. However, if the symbolic nature of the manifestation is understood and appreciated, it provides the seeker with a path to follow, a bridge that leads to the transcendent.

The second major issue humans face when trying to deal with the Divine is language. Human language grows out of human experience and provides us with symbols of shared meaning. In order for information to be shared by verbal or written language there must be a common fund of experience. This does not mean that all of us must have the same experiences to share meanings, but that we must have similar experiences or have shared similar stories or ideas. The human mind and imagination have the ability to discern patterns and concepts that allow us to generalize and organize the world around us, and to project our experience to encompass other people's experiences as well. But because language grows out of human experience, the language used to express human understanding of the Divine is faulty and imprecise. Even so, it makes possible the sharing of information and the growth of ideas and concepts which, even if inadequate, can help move people closer to the reality of the Divine. As long as the imprecision and inadequacy of the images shared is not forgotten, language raises all who participate in the efforts to improve their understanding of the mystery of the Divine.

Language grows out of human experience, but it also helps shape that experience over time. The large number and wide range of languages and dialects developed throughout the world testifies to the utility of language in culture. Each language reflects the values developed and preserved in the life of the people involved. Each language develops words for the concepts significant to the people's experiences, both mundane and spiritual, and while many may have equivalents in other languages, some may not. With respect to the Divine, the culture and its language precede efforts within the culture to develop a theology. While every known culture has some concept of spirituality, the development of a comprehensive theology seems to require a highly developed system of abstract thought. A people's theology grows out of an accumulation of personal experiences, but the ability to talk or write about experiences with the Divine comes after the basic framework of the language has been developed and people can share concepts and experiences. The categories of thought, the manner in which a culture organizes itself, determine the vocabulary available for dealing with the Divine as people struggle to put into words their experiences.

One example of the limitations of language in dealing with the Divine is gender. In human experience, persons, and other animals have gender. As awareness of the Divine develops, the personal nature of the Divine as manifest in the natural world increasingly emerges. Because the linguistic structures for persons within the language are gender specific, the predominant way cultures speak of and envision the Divine is also gender-laden. Cultures and religions differ as to whether their deity is male or female, and those religions with multiple expressions of the Divine usually have some of each. The enduring major world religions, with the notable exceptions of the indigenous Chinese religions Confucianism and Taoism have tended to assign maleness to the primary manifestation of the Divine while holding the transcendent Divine reality to be beyond gender. This is because the cultures in which the theology of religion developed were male-dominated. Although Chinese culture was also male-dominated, the manner in which Confucianism "backed into" religion through veneration of ancestors assured that the original ancestors would be both male and female. However, the "proper" role of women in Confucianism is that of subordination to men. Taoism tends to think of the Divine in less personal terms than other major religions and thereby avoids assigning gender. Yet even there the fundamental concept of the dynamic tension of opposites, yin and yang, while both essential and theoretically equal, assigns the female to the negative or passive side, with practical consequences that result in a suppression of women in the culture. Of the Eight Immortals representing divine attributes in Taoism, six are men and two women. The mutual reinforcement of a male-dominated culture and maleness being ascribed to deity has created one of the greatest distortions of human understanding of the Divine and one of the greatest misuses of religion in culture. By ascribing maleness to the primary manifestations of the Divine, the culture tends to approve of the subordination of women to men. Christianity has a particular problem in this regard which will be discussed below. The culprit is the human tendency to ascribe final reality concerning the Divine to the various manifestations of the Divine in the natural world.

The nature of the Divine remains a mystery to humankind, yet in every culture and time, some perception of the Divine forms the framework for human awareness of both the self and the natural world. We sense in both the imprint of some power or being much greater than ourselves, and we struggle to comprehend and relate to this Divine. The varieties of religions and philosophies developed by humankind testify both to the profusion and the subtlety of the manifestations of the Divine in the mundane world. The testimony of humankind through the ages is that the Divine is both profoundly Other and closer to each of us than our own self-conscious awareness. With St. Augustine we proclaim, "Our hearts are restless until we rest in Thee."[21]

---

[21] Augustine, *Confessions*, Book 1.

The Creation Myths

What we are looking for in these creation stories is a way of experiencing the world that will open to us the transcendent that informs it, and at the same time forms ourselves within it. That is what people want. That is what the soul asks for [22]
—Joseph Campbell

The creation myths of religions serve foundationally to explain the human condition. They seek to establish the nature of the relationship between the Creator who is the Divine, and the created world, especially the people who claim the particular myth. Eastern religions and most tribal religions tend to accept the basic material of this world as a given and focus on the organizing of the natural world and the creatures that inhabit it.[23] Western religions tend to include the creation of the material world as basic to their myths. All creation myths are symbolic in nature. They express in human, this-worldly terms activity and inten-

---

[22] Joseph Campbell, *The Power of Myth* (New York: Doubleday, 1988), 52.
[23] See Smith, *Forgotten Truth*, 122, footnote 2, for a fascinating anecdote concerning Buddhist/Hindu belief as shared by the Dalai Lama. The belief affirms the idea of existent physical reality that is in infinite cyclical change of formation, collapse and reformation.

tionality of the transcendent being or power by which the natural world and humankind were brought into being. They are myths precisely because they attempt to express in human language that which is beyond human comprehension or expression. They attempt to describe *what* happened, not *how* it happened. A great error of modern fundamentalists is to insist on a literal reading of their religious myths. A great error of modern religious liberals is to abandon the mythical, transcendent basis of their faith and restrict their interpretation of scripture and religious tradition to the non-transcendent world within which science operates. The task of modern theologians is to reclaim the mythical, transcendent basis of their faith and reframe it for modern people.

By and large, Christianity and Islam adopted the creation myth of Judaism as their own and adapted it to conform to their revelation of the Divine. This story briefly and symbolically tells of the creation of the natural world by God, either *ex nihilo* (from nothing) or *ex Dio* (from God). Deity is portrayed as personal, intentional, and moral. These myths do not deny the essential transcendent nature of the Divine, but they focus on the aspect of the Divine that relates to this world and humankind. The world human beings experience is understood to be a special part of the Divine creation, the full nature of which is presently beyond human understanding.

Pre-scientific Christianity, somewhere along its journey, lost sight of the nature and power of myth in orienting people to their place in the scheme of things. While some modern scholars blame this development on the Enlightenment and the rise of rationalism in Europe, in reality, both Roman and Eastern church leadership had already done this by asserting their authority as the exclusive connection between the Divine and human. This leadership, rather than affirming the myth and mediating the transcendent to the people, conceived of itself as the protectors of the Divine, guardians of the gates of Heaven the true nature of which was to be withheld from the masses who by their inherent sinfulness and ignorance were unable and unworthy to glimpse such glory. The Protestant Reformation challenged the authority of the Roman Church, but assumed the same functional stance, substituting their interpretation of Biblical scripture for the Catholic hierarchy tradition as authoritative. Except for the Christian mystics, both church leaders and the people grew to take literally the Genesis creation myth. Church leaders failed to see or appreciate the implications of such simplistic faith. This is in spite of the myth's internal logical inconsistencies such as the assertion that the sun and other heavenly bodies by which we measure days were not even created until the fourth "day." Simplistic interpretations of the myth by churchmen, such as the pronouncement that according to Biblical research creation took place about the year 4000 BCE, exacerbated the problem. Such literal interpretation of the myth was easily challenged and debunked by the emerging science of the Enlightenment. Many church leaders and theologians, then and now, failed to return to the spiritual roots of Christian theology and re-embrace the mythical language of the creation story of Genesis. Christian mystics, who consistently tried to convey the essentially transcendent basis of their visions, were marginalized. Roman Catholics continued to assert the authority of the traditional teaching of the church, and Protestants continued to assert the literal authority of the Bible to refute the emerging assertions of science. Science continued to pile up evidence of the evolutionary emergence of the natural world over eons of time; because the "what" of myth was presented by church leaders as the "how" of science, it became increasingly unbelievable to modern people.

According to modern biblical scholars, the Genesis account of creation was developed and passed down for generations as oral tradition by the early Hebrews. When committed to writing, it endeavored to combine at least two parallel accounts, a priestly version and a prophetic version. While both are mythical in nature, the first (Genesis 1—2:3 of the received text) focuses on the *ex nihilo* or *ex Dio* creation of the entire natural world and emphasizes the sacramental nature of creation. This first account follows, in broad essence, the sequence of what we understand to have been the evolution of the natural world. The second

(Genesis 2:4–24) focuses on the emergence of life from the barren earth and emphasizes the central role of humanity in God's plan for creation. This account asserts that man was the first living entity created. Plant and animal life were created to provide man with sustenance, with vocation, and with moral responsibility. After creating man, God provided plants to serve man's need for aesthetic sensibility and bodily survival. God then planted in a central place the tree of life and the tree of the knowledge of good and evil. The tree of life symbolizes man's eternal nature, man's eternal destiny. The tree of the knowledge of good and evil symbolizes man's moral responsibility, the necessity for man to have real choice with real consequences. What follows is the story of the temptation and fall of the first parents of humankind from obedience to God and their expulsion from the Garden of Eden into the mundane world with its cycles of life and death.

All three faiths—Judaism, Christianity and Islam—have looked to this creation myth as explanation for the evil in the world and humankind's precarious passage through it. Each has developed their understanding of how God acted to compensate for Adam and Eve's weakness in submitting to temptation. Each has struggled to justify the apparent flaw in God's perfect creation that allowed evil to assert itself. The story has been used to justify many social practices such as the subjugation of women, both because Eve derived from Adam and because she was the first to succumb to temptation and enticed Adam to succumb. For some in Christianity, the sin of Adam and Eve was seen as so grievous that the only way to balance the injustice of their disobedience was for God to send his sinless Only Begotten Son to suffer the injustice of mortal death as atonement. Many modern Christians have difficulty with the morality of such theology.

The temptation story raises other theological issues for Christians. The myth has one of the creatures that God created (and pronounced "good") enticing Eve to defy God and justifying her disobedience on the grounds that God did not disclose the true nature of the forbidden fruit. The talking serpent claims that God's warning that death will result from eating the fruit is false and that God's prohibition is intended to hide the real effect of this special fruit, namely that it will make humans like God in the sense that they will know good and evil. The serpent, of course tells Eve only a half-truth; by eating the forbidden fruit our first parents not only become aware of good and evil, they also become mortal. Prior to the pair's disobedience, the myth leaves open the question of human mortality. God also planted the Tree of Life in the garden, which implies that there was at least the possibility of never-ending life for them. God's response to their disobedience includes closing off Adam and Eve's access to the Tree of Life. The traditional story portrays God *reacting* to Adam and Eve's actions, not fully in control and seeing his creation become corrupted contrary to his intentions.

The question as to the source of the evil in the Garden of Eden is troubling to many Christians. Many interpret the serpent as representing Satan, or evil personified. The question then is whether God created Satan and how he came to spoil God's "good" creation. Another interpretation has man defying God and by willfulness asserting human ego in opposition to God's will. At issue is the fundamental concept of God as omnipotent, omniscient, and omni-beneficent, and humankind's fatally flawed nature. Did God create man good or essentially depraved? The idea that all humanity suffers from the bad choices of our first parents seems grossly unfair to most people. We hold that each of us should be responsible for our own choices and not those over which we have no control. Nevertheless, we are aware that in this life there is a great deal over which we have little or no control. God's good creation seems to many to be seriously flawed, and few are comfortable with the explanation provided by traditional interpretations of the creation myth we have inherited. Yet if we abandon our myth, as many have done, including theologians and philosophers, we are left with a diminished sense of who we are, and where we fit in the world in which we find ourselves.[24]

---

[24] "People have a profound need to believe that the truth they perceive is rooted in the unchanging depths of the universe; for were it not, could the truth be really important?" Smith, *Forgotten Truth*, v.

The Creation Myths

While it is true that creation myths were devised by people, in most cases we have little idea who these people were or how the particular form of a myth developed. We often assume that our myths arose out of revelatory experiences of wise leaders early in a people's history. The myths endure because they have met real needs over many generations. But what happens when a myth ceases to provide people with a valid way of embracing their existence? History has many examples of people, cultures, religions, even civilizations which have failed. While there may be many reasons for the fall of a people into obscurity and the death of their culture and religion, when this happens because of internal disintegration, a root cause is the failure of their myths to hold them together, to give them a sense of identity, purpose, and destiny. This could be because either the leaders failed to honor and live by the truth of the myth or the people found the myth to be increasingly irrelevant to the experiences of their lives.

As the nineteenth century dawned in Europe and the emerging United States of America, the creation myth of Christianity was being seriously undermined by the advance of the humanism of the Enlightenment and the optimism, even arrogance, of scientific and technological progress. Copernicus, Kepler, and Galileo had displaced the earth and its inhabitants from the center of the universe. Newton had hypothesized a clock-work universe, probably created by God but now left to run on its own. Science was "putting nature to the rack" to discover its laws, which were held to be completely rational, comprehensible, and subject to manipulation by human intelligence. The divine and mystical were viewed as products of ignorance, and religion was mere superstition which was exploited by churchmen for control of a gullible populace. As science continued to reveal the mechanics of the natural world, "Pascal recoiled in dread from the emptiness of the cosmos; Descartes saw the human being as the sole living denizen of an inert universe; Hobbs imagined God retreating from the world, and Nietzsche declared that God was dead: humanity had lost its orientation and was hurtling toward an infinite nothingness."[25] Christian leaders, when they reacted at all, buried their heads in the shifting sands of tradition and posited interpretations of Biblical myths and poetical expressions as scientific proofs and declarations of fact. These interpretations, not surprisingly, were becoming increasingly unsupportable.

Reframing the traditional creation myth of Judeo-Christianity for modern Western people is a daunting but essential task. A wide range of efforts have been made, from psychological to sociological to anthropological analyses, but they have not been very successful.[26] A significant problem is that myths are not rationally constructed but emerge from the collective consciousness of a culture. "The deepest definition of a civilization may indeed be that it is a form of life empowered by an embracing myth, but myths of this order cannot be created consciously. In some sense of the word, myths can only be revealed which may be what Heidegger had in mind when toward the close of his life he said that 'only a god can save us now.'"[27]

---

[25] Armstrong, *The Battle for God*, 365.
[26] See Smith, *Beyond the Post-Modern Mind*, for discussions on the roles of theses fields of science in both deconstructing and attempting to displace the traditional myths as a source of orientation for modern humanity.
[27] Smith, *Beyond the Post-Modern Mind*, 20.

A New Creation Myth

Whence all creation had its origin, he, whether he fashioned it or whether he did not, he who surveys it all from highest heaven, he knows – or maybe even he does not know. [28]

—Vedic Hymn

Far from the academic world and the ecclesiastical corridors of power, the nineteenth-century American prophet Joseph Smith Jr.[29] had a series of visions in 1830 which provide a somewhat

---

[28] Quoted in Novak, *The World's Wisdom*, 7.
[29] Joseph Smith, Jr. (1805–1844) was a marginally-educated farm boy raised on the frontier of an expanding United States of America. At the age of fourteen he claimed to have had a vision of an encounter with Jesus Christ in response to his prayerful struggle to know which of the many versions of Christianity he should follow. This epiphany was followed by a series of angelic visitations and his commission to translate from a collection of "golden" plates the religious history and theology of ancient migrants to the Americas, known as the Book of Mormon (published in 1830). He subsequently organized a religious movement initially intended to restore primitive Christianity. In this movement, he functioned as a prophet claiming to receive instruction and insight from God in all aspects of life. He and his followers attempted to establish religious communities but suffered constant opposition from non-believers and both official and sponta-

Divine Providence: God's Plan for Humankind

different understanding of the foundational creation myth of Judaism, Christianity and Islam. It is a recasting of the myth that can serve as the basis for refocusing Christianity to serve humankind in the modern world. Unknown except to his small band of followers and soon largely forgotten or unappreciated, apparently even by Smith himself,[30] this version was published by his son in 1865.[31] The myth is cast as a spiritual experience

---

neous persecution from local populations and governments due to intolerance on both sides. Smith's early fundamental Christianity gradually gave way to millennialism and increasingly Gnostic/ritualistic practices, causing serious internal strife and dissension within the church. Smith was killed by a mob in 1844 and the church split into numerous factions. Two major factions survive currently: The Church of Jesus Christ of Latter-day Saints (Mormons) based in Salt Lake City, Utah, and the Community of Christ (formerly known as The Reorganized Church of Jesus Christ of Latter Day Saints), based in Independence, Missouri. The Mormon Church has built its theology and practice on Smith's later, ritual-based teaching, while the Community of Christ maintains his earlier mainline Christian beliefs and practices.

[30] It is important to note that any and all pronouncements by those claiming to be speaking for the Divine must stand on their own merits in the larger context in which they are given. The pronouncements neither convey special status on the prophet, nor should they be given greater credence because of the status or reputation of the prophet. True revelations are expressions of divine insight, the meaning and significance of which may or may not be fully appreciated by the human spokesperson. Thus I do not claim any special status for Joseph Smith Jr. or the churches he founded; his "prophetic" work was sporadic and often contradictory, as was his life.

[31] The visions were published in church periodicals of the time, but not as a recasting of the foundational creation myth of the Old Testament. Smith did create a manuscript of a reworking of the entire Bible with these visions as its starting point but seems to have lost interest in it and never had it published in his lifetime. The manuscript was retained by his widow Emma, the mother of Joseph Smith III, who became the leader in 1860 of the faction presently known as Community of Christ. Joseph III obtained the manuscript from Emma and headed an editing committee that produced a Bible version known as the Joseph Smith Translation or, more commonly, as the Inspired Version of the Bible (abbreviated in future references as IV). It was first published in 1865 by the Reorganized Church of Jesus Christ of Latter Day Saints (Community of Christ), which continues to publish it as The Holy Scriptures. The Mormon Church also publishes the visions as the Book of Moses, a part of their Pearl of Great Price.

A New Creation Myth

of the Hebrew Prophet Moses and relates an encounter with God and the subsequent prophetic visions he experienced.

Genesis Chapter 1

"And it came to pass that the Lord spake unto Moses, saying, Behold, I reveal unto you concerning this heaven and this earth; write the words which I speak.

I am the Beginning and the End; the Almighty God; By mine Only Begotten I created these things.

Yea, in the beginning I created the heaven, and the earth upon which thou standest.

And the earth was without form, and void; and I caused darkness to come up upon the face of the deep.

And my Spirit moved upon the face of the waters, for I am God.

And I, God, said, Let there be light, and there was light.

and I, God, saw the light, and that light was good. And I, God, divided the light from the darkness.

And I, God, called the light day, and the darkness I called night. And this I did by the word of my power; and it was done as I spake. And the evening and the morning were the first day.

And again, I, God, said, Let there be a firmament in the midst of the waters; and it was so, even as I spake. And I said, Let it divide the waters from the waters; and it was done.

And I, God, made the firmament, and divided the waters; yea, the great waters under the firmament, from the waters which were above the firmament; and it was so, even as I spake.

And I, God, called the firmament heaven. And the evening and the morning were the second day.

Divine Providence: God's Plan for Humankind

And I, God, said, Let the waters under the heaven be gathered into one place; and it was so. And I, God, said, Let there be dry land; and it was so.

And I, God, called the dry land earth; and the gathering together of the waters called I the sea.

And I, God, saw that all things which I had made were good.

And I, God, said, Let the earth bring forth grass; the herb yielding seed; the fruit tree yielding fruit after his kind; and the tree yielding fruit, whose seed should be in itself, upon the earth; and it was so, even as I spake.

And the earth brought forth grass; every herb yielding seed after his kind; and the tree yielding fruit, whose seed should be in itself, after his kind.

And I, God, saw that all things which I had made were good. And the evening and the morning were the third day.

And I, God, said, Let there be lights in the firmament of heaven, to divide the day from the night; and let them be for signs and for seasons, and for days and for years, and let them be for lights in the firmament of the heaven, to give light upon the earth; and it was so.

And I, God, made two great lights; the greater light to rule the day, and the lesser light to rule the night; and the greater light was the sun, and the lesser light was the moon.

And the stars also were made, even according to my word; and I, God, set them in the firmament of the heaven, to give light upon the earth; the sun to rule over the day, and the moon to rule over the night, and to divide the light from the darkness.

And I, God, saw that all things which I had made were good. And the evening and the morning were the fourth day.

A New Creation Myth

And I, God, said, Let the waters bring forth abundantly, the moving creatures that hath life, and fowl which may fly above the earth, in the open firmament of heaven.

And I, God, created great whales, and every living creature that moveth, which the waters brought forth abundantly, after their kind; and every winged fowl, after his kind.

And I, God, saw that all things which I had created were good; and I, God, blessed them, saying, Be fruitful, and multiply, and fill the waters in the sea, and let the fowl multiply in the earth. And the evening and the morning were the fifth day.

And I, God, said, Let the earth bring forth the living creature, after his kind; cattle and creeping things, and beasts of the earth, after their kind; and it was so.

And I, God, made the beasts of the earth, after their kind; and cattle after their kind; and everything which creepeth upon the earth, after his kind. And I, God, saw that all these things were good.

And I, God, said unto mine Only Begotten, which was with me from the beginning, Let us make man in our image, after our likeness; and it was so.

And I, God, said, Let them have dominion over the fishes of the sea, and over the fowl of the air, and over the cattle, and over all the earth, and over every creeping thing that creepeth upon the earth.

And I, God, created man in mine own image, in the image of mine Only Begotten created I him; male and female created I them.

And I, God, blessed them and said unto them, Be fruitful, and multiply, and replenish the earth, and subdue it; and have dominion over the fish of the sea, and over the fowl of the air, and over every living thing that moveth upon the earth.

And I, God, said unto man, Behold, I have given you every herb, bearing seed, which is upon the face of all the earth; and every tree in the which shall be the fruit of a tree, yielding seed; to you it shall be for meat.

And to every beast of the earth, and to every fowl of the air, and to everything that creepeth upon the earth, wherein I grant life, there shall be given every clean herb for meat; and it was so, even as I spake.

And I, God, saw everything that I had made, and behold, all things which I had made were very good. And the evening and the morning were the sixth day."

Genesis Chapter 2: 1 - 12

"Thus the heavens and the earth were finished, and all the host of them.

And on the seventh day, I, God, ended my work, and all things which I had made; and I rested on the seventh day from all my work; and all things which I had made were finished. And I, God, saw that they were good.

And I, God, blessed the seventh day, and sanctified it, because that in it I had rested from all my work, which I, God, had created and made.

And now, behold, I say unto you, that these are the generations of the heaven, and of the earth, when they were created in the day that I the Lord God made the heaven and the earth, and every plant of the field before it was in the earth, and every herb of the field before it grew;

For I, the Lord God, created all things of which I have spoken, spiritually, before they were naturally upon the face of the earth; for I, the Lord God, had not caused it to rain upon the face of the earth.

A New Creation Myth

> And I, the Lord God, had created all the children of men, and not yet a man to till the ground, for in heaven created I them, and there was not yet flesh upon the earth, neither in the water, neither in the air;
>
> But I, the Lord God, spake, and there went up a mist from the earth, and watered the whole face of the ground.
>
> And I, the Lord God, formed man from the dust of the ground, and breathed into his nostrils the breath of life; and man became a living soul; the first flesh upon the earth, the first man also;
>
> Nevertheless, all things were before created, but spiritually were they created and made, according to my word.
>
> And I, the Lord God, planted a garden eastward in Eden; and there I put the man whom I had formed.
>
> And out of the ground, made I, the Lord God, to grow every tree naturally, that is pleasant to the sight of man, and man could behold it, and it became also a living soul; for it was spiritual in the day I created it; for it remaineth in the sphere in which I, God, created it; yea, even all things which I prepared for the use of man; and man saw that it was good for food.
>
> And I, the Lord God, planted the tree of life also, in the midst of the garden; and also the tree of knowledge of good and evil."[32]

The account has several significant aspects:

- The tradition that Moses was the author of the creation myth and the rest of the Torah, or Pentateuch, is affirmed. The point is not to bolster this tradition, which is largely discounted as historically accurate by modern scholars. Rather it confirms

---

[32] Genesis 1:1—2:12 IV.

the mythical character of the visions, both Smith's and that of Moses, which is related by Smith. The unknown writers or transcribers of the Torah invoked the status of Moses, the greatest of the Hebrew prophets, to give it credence and authority. In doing so they affirm the thrust and focus of the teaching of Moses in the oral tradition and assert the prophetic character of the myth. It is interesting to note that Smith's version is presented in first person rather than the third person of the traditional account. This also emphasizes the prophetic nature of the myth.

- Smith's recasting of the myth presents not two different accounts of the natural creation, which in the received text is a somewhat awkward blending of priestly and prophetic strains from the oral tradition, but two creations: the first a spiritual creation, and, subsequently, the natural creation. This two-stage creation emphasizes the primacy of the spiritual over the material, not only in terms of sequence but also in terms of derivation; the material world is dependent on prior spiritual existence. This ordering of creation affirms the foundational theological premises of all the major religious faiths[33]—that the Divine is, in its essence, spiritual, and it is the spiritual aspect of humankind and all of the natural world that is basic and eternal.

- In this creation myth, humans are the first creatures made by God. The primacy of the spiritual creation of humankind suggests that the material world was made to be the venue for the activity of human beings. This interpretation is not just a display of human ego but is an essential focus for the illumination of the mythical purpose of the creation story: to provide a basic orientation for humanity, their place in the scheme of things. In the spiritual creation process, which occurs in God's essential realm, this sequence is not illogical. The account of the ordered creation places humankind in its proper developmental sequence. It should be noted that humanity is created in the image of God; male and female are both in the image of God. Thus, exclusive male images of the Divine are inherently limited.

---

[33] Smith, *Forgotten Truth*.

A New Creation Myth

- The garden seems to have been created to provide everything humans need to sustain and enjoy life. Most significantly, God placed in the garden two symbols not connected with the sustaining of mortal life, the tree of life and the tree of knowledge of good and evil. The tree of life provides for human immortality, should they choose it. But the tree of the knowledge of good and evil provides the possibility of human free will. Free will requires the possibility of more than one option, and morality requires that options be degrees of goodness. It makes no sense to call something good if there is no possibility that something else is other than good or at least less good.

The myth to this point has dealt with the creation process, spiritually and naturally, and has provided for the possibility of moral choice. The focus then turns directly to the issue of free will and moral responsibility.

Genesis 2:18 - 31

"And I, the Lord God, took the man, and put him into the garden of Eden, to dress it, and to keep it.

And I, the Lord God, commanded the man, saying, Of every tree of the garden thou mayest freely eat;

But of the tree of the knowledge of good and evil, thou shalt not eat of it;

Nevertheless, thou mayest choose for thyself, for it is given unto thee; but remember that I forbid it;

For in the day thou eatest thereof thou shalt surely die.

And I, the Lord God, said unto mine Only Begotten, that it was not good that the man should be alone;

Wherefore, I will make an help meet for him.

And out of the ground, I the Lord God, formed every beast of the field, and every fowl of the air;

Divine Providence: God's Plan for Humankind

and commanded that they should come unto Adam, to see what he would call them.

And they were also living souls; for I, God, breathed into them the breath of life, and commanded that whatsoever Adam called every living creature, that should be the name thereof.

And Adam gave names to all cattle, and to the fowl of the air, and to every beast of the field; but as for Adam, there was not found an help meet for him.

And I, the Lord God, caused a deep sleep to fall upon Adam, and he slept, and I took one of his ribs, and closed up the flesh in the stead thereof; and the rib, which I, the Lord God had taken from man, made I a woman, and brought her unto the man.

And Adam said, This I know now is bone of my bones, and flesh of my flesh. She shall be called woman, because she was taken out of man.

Therefore shall a man leave his father and his mother, and shall cleave unto his wife; and they shall be one flesh.

And they were both naked, the man and his wife, and were not ashamed.[34]

- Having placed man in the garden with options, God proceeds to give instructions concerning the options. God commands man not to eat the fruit of the tree of knowledge of good and evil and states the result of eating of this tree. But he also says that man may choose for himself whether to eat this fruit or not. This setup makes possible man's exercise of free will.

- But is free choice really moral choice when the chooser is ignorant of the consequences? In the myth, man is created by God, in the presence of God, and amidst God's good creation. Since he has no experience of anything other than good, can he comprehend evil in any fashion? Though threatened with death for disobeying God's commandment, can man comprehend the

---

[34] Genesis 2:18-31 IV.

threat? Rather, man in this state is truly innocent. He has no concept of evil or death. How then can moral choice really function? Rather than presenting man in the Garden as perfect, this myth presents man as innocent, not yet fully formed in the image of God, but with the potential to become free and moral.

- This part of the myth also introduces language in the naming of the creatures by man, and the concept of marriage as a cleaving together of man and woman is introduced.

The next part of the myth is an extensive elaboration on the temptation event.

Genesis 3

"And I, the Lord God, spake unto Moses, saying, That Satan whom thou hast commanded in the name of mine Only Begotten, is the same which was from the beginning;

And he came before me, saying, Behold I, send me, I will be thy Son, and I will redeem all mankind, that one soul shall not be lost, and surely I will do it; wherefore, give me thine honor.

But behold, my beloved Son, which was my beloved and chosen from the beginning, said unto me: Father, thy will be done, and the glory be thine forever.

Wherefore, because that Satan rebelled against me, and sought to destroy the agency of man, which I, the Lord God, had given him; and also that I should give unto him mine own power; by the power of mine Only Begotten I caused that he should be cast down; and he became Satan.

Yea, even the devil, the father of all lies, to deceive, and to blind men, and to lead them captive at his will, even as many as would not hearken unto my voice.

And now, the serpent was more subtle than any beast of the field, which I, the Lord God, had made.

Divine Providence: God's Plan for Humankind

And Satan put into the heart of the serpent, for he had drawn away many after him; and he sought also to beguile Eve, for he knew not the mind of God; wherefore, he sought to destroy the world.

And he said unto the woman, Yea, hath God said, Ye shall not eat of every tree of the garden. And he spake by the mouth of the serpent.

And the woman said unto the serpent, We may eat of the fruit of the trees of the garden; but of the fruit of the tree which thou beholdest in the midst of the garden, God hath said, Ye shall not eat of it, neither shall ye touch it, lest ye die.

And the serpent said unto the woman, Ye shall not surely die; for God doth know, that in the day ye eat thereof, then your eyes shall be opened, and ye shall be as gods, knowing good and evil.

And when the woman saw that the tree was good for food, and that it became pleasant to the eyes, and a tree to be desired to make her wise, she took of the fruit thereof, and did eat; and gave also unto her husband with her, and he did eat.

And the eyes of them both were opened, and they knew that they had been naked, and they sewed fig leaves together, and made themselves aprons.

And they heard the voice of the Lord God, as they were walking in the garden, in the cool of the day.

And Adam and his wife went to hide themselves from the presence of the Lord God, amongst the trees of the garden.

And I, the Lord God, called unto Adam, and said unto him, Where goest thou? And he said, I heard thy voice, in the garden, and I was afraid, because I beheld that I was naked, and I hid myself.

And I, the Lord God, said unto Adam, Who told thee that thou wast naked? Hast thou eaten of the

A New Creation Myth

tree whereof I commanded thee that thou shouldst not eat, if so thou shouldst surely die?

And the man said, The woman whom thou gavest me, and commanded that she should remain with me, she gave me of the fruit of the tree, and I did eat.

And I, the Lord God, said unto the woman, What is this thing which thou hast done?

And the woman said, The serpent beguiled me, and I did eat.

And I, the Lord God, said unto the serpent, Because thou hast done this, thou shalt be cursed above all cattle, and above every beast of the field; upon thy belly shalt thou go, and dust shalt thou eat all the days of thy life;

And I will put enmity between thee and the woman; between thy seed and her seed; and he shall bruise thy head, and thou shalt bruise his heel.

Unto the woman, I, the Lord God, said, I will greatly multiply thy sorrow, and thy conception; in sorrow thou shalt bring forth children, and thy desire shall be to thy husband, and he shall rule over thee.

And unto Adam, I, the Lord God, said, Because thou has hearkened unto the voice of thy wife, and hast eaten of the fruit of the tree, of which I commanded thee, saying, Thou shalt not eat of it, cursed shall be the ground for thy sake; in sorrow shalt thou eat of it all the days of thy life;

Thorns also and thistles shall it bring forth to thee; and thou shalt eat the herb of the field;

By the sweat of thy face shalt thou eat bread, until thou shalt return unto the ground, for thou shalt surely die; for out of it wast thou taken, for dust thou wast, and unto dust shalt thou return.

And Adam called his wife's name Eve, because she was the mother of all living; For thus have I, the

Divine Providence: God's Plan for Humankind

Lord God, called the first of all women, which are many.

Unto Adam, and also unto his wife, did I, the Lord God, make coats of skins, and clothed them.

And I, the Lord God, said unto mine Only Begotten, Behold, the man is become as one of us, to know good and evil; and now, lest he put forth his hand, and partake also of the tree of life, and eat, and live forever;

Therefore, I, the Lord God, will send him forth from the garden of Eden, to till the ground from whence he was taken;

For, as I, the Lord God, liveth, even so my words cannot return void, for, as they go forth out of my mouth, they must be fulfilled.

So I drove out the man, and I placed at the east of the garden of Eden, cherubim, and a flaming sword, which turned every way, to keep the way of the tree of life."[35]

- The pre-existence of Satan and of the Only Begotten Son of God, while implied in other Christian scriptural texts, is stated explicitly in Smith's recasting of the creation myth. These concepts are foreign to the Jewish tradition or Islam's reading of the myth. The Gospel of John in the received text identifies creation with the Word, which Christians understand to mean the Son of God who became incarnate in Jesus Christ.

- Much of Christian theology glosses over the implications of the idea of a beginning. When pushed, traditional theologians will say that included in the creation of the material world is the creation of time. The term, "in the beginning" means the point at which time starts to function. There is no time before this beginning. Human beings have difficulty conceptualizing existence outside of time, but this is what is indicated in the creation myth. What exists outside of time is called eternity, but to most people

---

[35] Genesis 3:1-31 IV.

A New Creation Myth

eternity just means endless time. While we may not be able to comprehend the idea of existence without time, we can entertain and work with the idea. In the New Testament book of Revelation, also highly mythical in nature, the end of natural existence as we know it is also presented as the end of time. The concept is that time is "contained" in eternity, but eternity is not restricted by time. For our comprehension, what occurs outside of time still may have sequence, cause and effect. Clearly, we cannot force the myth into our logic framework, and we would be unwise to try. But we can use the myth to understand *what* happened and at least some of the *why*.

- While many theologians over the centuries have interpreted the temptation of Eve as the work of Satan, this has been based on reading back into the myth concepts introduced much later in the received text. Smith's recasting of the myth provides not only a clear statement of Satan as the instigator of the temptation, but also an explanation of the origin and function of Satan. In the Old Testament he is sometimes presented as an agent of God whose function was to tempt and test human beings. In the New Testament, he is presented as an independent adversary bent on thwarting the plan of God for the redemption of humankind. He is credited as being the leader of other fallen angels, the prince of this world and the prince of darkness, a tempter of humankind, and an adversary of the prophets and of Jesus himself. In the end of human history, he is mythically to lead the forces of evil in a great battle for the souls of human beings and will be defeated and cast into outer darkness with all his followers

- Smith's telling of the myth states that the proximate cause for Satan's rebellion was the issue of who would redeem humankind from their estrangement from God. Satan offers to perform this function by overpowering the free will of humankind and bringing all people into submission to the rule of God, but this program would destroy human agency. Such a development would destroy the essential nature of human beings as God wished to create them. Instead, the Son of God offers to redeem humankind by sacrificing himself, facilitating the reconciliation

Divine Providence: God's Plan for Humankind

of humankind to God by their own free will but with the prospect that some may choose otherwise.

- While the general parameters of the plan of redemption are known to all Christians, the sequence in Smith's recasting of the myth is different. The myth places the rebellion of Satan over the redemption of humankind *prior* to the creation and fall. This means that the fall of man was no accident or mistake. Not only was it known to God before it occurred, but it is an essential part of God's creation process. In order for human beings to become free beings in their own right, it is necessary for them to experience separation from God; to know good and evil; to be responsible for the moral choices they make, choices with real consequences. This can only occur in neutral territory, in a situation in which the power and glory of God are not overwhelming, and other possibilities for human existence can be seen as viable by individual human beings.

- Satan's role in Smith's myth is more direct and explicit than in the received text. He serves as the impetus for the Adam and Eve's eating of the forbidden fruit. The possibility of their eating the fruit was there from the time it was within their reach. God created the forbidden fruit, specifically commanded it be left untouched, and explained the consequences of their choosing to disobey the commandment. But explicit temptation seems to have been required for the humans to focus on it. What Satan does is awaken their self-awareness by suggesting that it is in their self-interest to make the fatal choice. While the eating of the forbidden fruit furthers God's program for humanity, it also is essential for Satan's program to establish his own following in opposition to God. This is, of course, the essence of Satan's rebellion in the first place: his choice to assert his independence from God which is the essence of sin. It is important to understand, however, that the choice for Adam and Eve is one of innocence for which they cannot be held morally responsible. With no understanding of disobedience, evil, or death, our mythical parents had no basis for moral choice. This does not mean that they could avoid the consequences of their disobedience, but rather that they cannot be blamed for having chosen as they did.

Smith's elaboration of the myth continues, making explicit the significance of moral choice in human creation.

Genesis 4

"And it came to pass, that after I, the Lord God, had driven them out, that Adam began to till the earth, and to have dominion over all the beasts of the field, and to eat his bread by the sweat of his brow, as I, the Lord had commanded him, and Eve also, his wife, did labor with him.

And Adam knew his wife, and she bare unto him sons and daughters, and they began to multiply, and to replenish the earth.

And from that time forth, the sons and daughters of Adam began to divide, two and two, in the land, and to till the land, and to tend flocks; and they also begat sons and daughters.

And Adam called upon the name of the Lord, and Eve also, his wife; and they heard the voice of the Lord, from the way towards the garden of Eden, speaking unto them, and they saw him not; for they were shut out from his presence.

And he gave unto them commandments, that they should worship the Lord their God; and should offer the firstlings of their flocks for an offering unto the Lord.

And Adam was obedient unto the commandments of the Lord. And after many days, an angel of the Lord appeared unto Adam, saying, Why dost thou offer sacrifices unto the Lord? And Adam said unto him, I know not, save the Lord commanded me.

And then the angel spake, saying, This thing is a similitude of the sacrifice of the Only Begotten of the Father, which is full of grace and truth;

Divine Providence: God's Plan for Humankind

Wherefore, thou shalt do all that thou doest, in the name of the Son. And thou shalt repent, and call upon God, in the name of the Son for evermore.

And in that day, the Holy Ghost fell upon Adam, which beareth record of the Father and the Son, saying, I am the Only Begotten of the Father from the beginning, henceforth and forever; that, as thou hast fallen, thou mayest be redeemed, and all mankind, even as many as will.

And in that day Adam blessed God, and was filled, and began to prophesy concerning all the families of the earth; saying, Blessed be the name of God, for, because of my transgression my eyes are opened, and in this life I shall have joy, and again, in the flesh I shall see God.

And Eve, his wife, heard all these things and was glad, saying, Were it not for our transgression, we never should have had seed, and never should have known good and evil, and the joy of our redemption, and the eternal life which God giveth unto all the obedient.

And Adam and Eve blessed the name of God; and they made all things known unto their sons and their daughters.

And Satan came among them, saying, I am also a son of God, and he commanded them, saying, Believe it not. And they believed it not; and they loved Satan more than God. And men began from that time forth to be carnal, sensual and devilish.[36]

- This elaboration of the creation myth makes it uniquely Christian and provides the framework for the complete scope of Christian divine providence. Adam and Eve, representing humankind, have become self-conscious, responsible for their daily survival, and faced with having to choose from both good and

---

[36] Genesis 4:1-13 IV.

evil. They have become separate from God but retain their sense of the divine presence. The Holy Ghost, God's spiritual presence, is abroad in the natural world to testify of the Divine, but Satan, the presence of evil, is also in the world to draw humankind away from the Divine by focusing them on themselves and their material world. Neither force is overwhelming; human beings must use all their faculties to discern their best course.

 - The role of the Son of God in the redemption of humanity is central to the divine plan. Unlike the Eastern religions where it is the responsibility of each individual to discover the essentially impersonal nature of the Divine, Christianity asserts that the essence of redemption is the establishment of a relationship between the individual and God. What was lost in the fall of Adam and Eve was innocence, yes, but more importantly they lost their direct relationship with God. By choosing to disobey God's commandment, they asserted their independence and placed their personal interest above that of their creator. Notwithstanding the innocence with which the estrangement was effected, the result is the same. The divine plan is for the estrangement to be temporary; the fulfillment of human creation is the reconciliation of human beings to God by their own free will. The witness of the Holy Ghost and of angelic messengers from God testifying of the existence of God and the Son of God is God's way of assuring that all persons have the option of developing a relationship with the Divine. However, the full nature of the relationship is dependent on God becoming accessible in personal, relational terms. The nature of God as creator is that the work toward the completion of creation, i.e. the reconciliation of humankind to the Divine of their own free will, requires the active involvement of God in the human condition. The incarnation of God in the person of Jesus Christ is essential to this reconciliation. In Christianity the initiative for Divine-human reconciliation lies with God; this is divine grace. But the process also requires human response by freely accepting their place as creature. This is Christian faith, expressed in Christian works.

 - The institution of worship of God by human beings is, first of all, this acknowledgement by humankind of its status as creatures and God as creator. Secondly, it is recognition that human happiness and fulfillment lies in their proper relationship with God. Such relationship requires conscious action by humankind.

- The creation myth presents the Son of God as a separate being from God the Father. Christianity has struggled with this issue from its earliest days. At this point, the myth is attempting to provide a handle for humankind on issues beyond human comprehension. This way of thinking about the Divine is useful for our comprehension of the other theological concepts expressed by the myth, but it should not be adopted literally without qualification. From the human perspective the Divine appears to have the nature of two beings. This concept will be discussed further in consideration of the Christian doctrine of the Trinity.

- The concept and practice of sacrifice in worship has played an often misunderstood and tragic role in many religions over the centuries. Human agendas and values often crept into the practices. Seeking greater control over natural forces affecting the lives of their people, priests in some cultures were inclined to increase the value of the sacrifices, first in numbers, and finally from vegetable and animal to human. The Christian understanding derived from the Jewish in which animal sacrifices symbolized atonement for the sins of the people. Jewish prophets were kept busy reigning in the excesses of the priests and reminding the nation of the symbolic and moral nature of the sacrifices. For Christians, the incarnation of God the Son, his life and death as Jesus of Nazareth, and his resurrection replaced the symbolism of animal sacrifices.

- Early Christian theologians and apologists, including the Apostle Paul, identified the crucifixion of Jesus as serving a similar atonement purpose but covering the entirety of humanity from Adam. However, the focus that God required a blood sacrifice for Adam's mythical sin in order to forgive humanity for becoming estranged from God was developed in the later context of Greek and Roman cultures. This focus has become increasingly unpalatable for many modern Christians. It is a concept that divides the more fundamentalist Christians from those deemed more liberal. While the death and resurrection of Jesus is at the heart of the Christian gospel, the scriptures focus on the life and ministry of the Son of God incarnate for human inspiration and instruction. The death of Jesus proved his humanity, but the resurrection proved his divinity. It was his coming into the material world that demonstrated God's love for humankind; the real sacrifice of the Only Begotten Son was his willingness to become separated from the Father, not the manner in which he regained the divine presence. Our human propensity to attribute human values to the Divine tends to shift our focus from the life of Jesus to his death as the primary expression of God's love. For mortal humans, physical death is the ultimate sacrifice, but for spiritual beings resident in the presence of God, separation from that presence, which can be termed spiritual death, is a greater sacrifice. Smith's version of the creation myth reminds us that the redemption of humanity from their separation from God was part of the divine plan of creation from before the beginning of this world; the incarnation and ministry of the Son of God was an essential element of the plan before it was initiated.

The creation myth presented to us through Joseph Smith retells the traditional myth in ways that do not contradict the earlier story itself, but it expands and refocuses the predominant interpretations and subsequent implications of the myth developed by theologians throughout the history of Christianity. Though there is original sin, there is no original guilt, nor the implication of innate depravity in humankind. Rather, each of us is a work in progress with the hope of becoming all that our Creator intends for us.

The Natural World

Tyger! Tyger! Burning bright in the forests of the night,
What immortal hand or eye could frame thy fearful symmetry? [37]

—William Blake

The creation myth outlined in the last chapter introduces a view of the natural world different from that described by science, the pervasive paradigm of modern Western civilization. But it is not opposed to science. Rather it puts science in a subordinate position instead of the dominant position modernity often claims. Science enables us to investigate the natural world, and to do so remarkably well. However, the creation myths and the sensibility of humankind affirm a spiritual reality beyond and superior to the natural world.[38] Through science we are able to discover much about the way the natural world functions and how it may be controlled and manipulated to serve our needs and desires. But science does not, and cannot, tell us why the natural world

---

[37] *A Treasury of the World's Best Loved Poems*, 30.
[38] See Smith, *Forgotten Truth,* for a profound and well-documented exploration of this topic.

is as it is or explain its origin or its meaning. As with many things in the natural world, science and its extension, technology, can be positive or negative, depending on how people use them. On the positive side, they allow human beings to achieve a measure of control over their environment, to ease labor, meet many needs, and within narrow limits prolong lives. On the negative side, they facilitate the control of the many by the few, the destruction of environment, and the potential for the destruction of all living things. More importantly perhaps, especially in the modern Western world, science and technology have tended to make people arrogant and self-absorbed, claiming for ourselves powers unwarranted by the reality of mortal life. Many in our society have adopted science as the only way of knowing about reality, and so decided that anything science cannot tell us is either unimportant or unknowable.[39]

The views of the natural world espoused by the world's religions vary in detail, but all affirm basic truths.[40] Buddhism takes the view that the essential nature of the natural world is to cause suffering for all people. Mortal life is characterized by suffering, decrepitude, and death. Buddhism teaches methods for dealing with this unpleasant but inevitable fact. The Four Noble Truths, the basis of Buddhist teaching, are

1. Life is suffering.
2. Suffering is caused by selfish desires.
3. Suffering can be overcome by mastering selfish desires.
4. Selfish desires can be mastered by following the Eightfold Path.

The Eightfold Path is Buddhism's set of disciplines for dealing with a hostile world. The disciplines teach self-control and focusing on the good of others rather than subjecting others and the natural world to one's selfish desires. Buddhism does not

---

[39] Smith, *Forgotten Truth,* chapter 5.
[40] See Huston Smith, *The World's Religions* (New York: HarperSanFrancisco, 1991) for a readable and sympathetic exploration of the major religious faiths. The brief generalities of the non-Christian religions in this paper are derived mainly from this book.

address the question of how the natural world came to be, or to be the way it is. Rather, it tends to adopt the Hindu perspective out of which it came. It accepts the natural world as a given and seeks to help people escape from its horrors and limitations. It posits no creator in the sense of a being who cares for creatures and wills their benefit. The goal of the Buddhist is to extinguish the self in the sea of total realization of being. That condition is both beyond the human ability to express and beyond the natural world to contain. Some forms of Buddhism focus on personal release and others on mutual help in seeking release, but none posits an ultimate Reality with personal traits such as love, compassion, judgment, and mercy. In Buddhism, the person who breaks through to the reality of the Divine may become the bridge for others; by following their example, people may follow the path more confidently. The first to achieve this, Siddhartha Gautama, became the Buddha, the Enlightened One. Although he did not seek such status, he is worshipped as a deity. The characteristics of all who achieve enlightenment are similar to those attributed to Deity in other faiths. Those who achieve some mastery in dealing with life develop and express these traits. Thus, Buddhism's view of the character of the natural world, while sobering as compared to other perspectives, is correct. Its view may not be satisfying for many, but its focus on the finitude and hurtful aspects of this world serves its purpose of helping people deal with life as they find it in a positive manner. The elements of compassion and the requirement of personal choice align Buddhism and some expressions of Christianity.

Hinduism espouses two primary and differing views of the natural world. It is divided over whether the natural world is real or unreal. In both cases, however, the natural world is an elaborate stage set devised by Divinity to provide the necessary challenges for humankind to develop its humanity and eventually claim its divine nature. Those who view this world as unreal seek to expose its ephemeral character and render it powerless. Those who assert the reality of the natural world still seek to eventually leave it behind as they pass from it to the higher reality of the divine presence. The Divine is the real force animating

The Natural World

all living things, but it is deeply hidden beneath multiple layers of "relatively real" material that reflect something of the nature of the divine. The essential core of being in each person is the divine essence. It is the job of each individual to peel away the layers of superficiality to reveal the real.

The Divine is passive with respect to the natural world and humankind's struggle to find their way out of the maze of transitory reality. The law of Karma, an impersonal but pervasive, moral cause and effect regulator, rewards or punishes individuals for positive or negative choices. According to Hindu cosmology, the natural world is spun out of the Divine from nothing, exists for a time, then collapses back to nothing. The cycle repeats endlessly, and the duration of each cycle is unimaginably long from the human point of view. The process resembles some readings of the big bang theory of modern astrophysics. Hinduism affirms that the cause of the natural world is the Divine which is immutable throughout the process. The fundamental elements of the essentially spiritual nature of the natural world and the requirement for humans to choose to become reconciled to this reality align Hinduism and some forms of Christianity.

The Chinese religions, Confucianism and Taoism, approach the natural world simply as a given, with neither positing a creation myth to explain it. Confucianism started simply as an ethical system for the management of social/political life and backed into a world view over many generations. The spiritual realm of Confucianism concerns only the ancestors of the Chinese people and is concerned only with the management of human life given the natural world that provides the context for it. Most Confucianists also embrace another religion, usually Taoism and/or Buddhism to cover the areas of human life not addressed by Confucianism. However, moral behavior and well-being in Confucianism also depend on people making the right choices in life.

Taoism views the natural world as the expression of the Life Force or Tao. The Tao is the ultimate reality, the reality of the natural world, and the true nature of each human being. It is each person's responsibility to appreciate this situation and allow

Divine Providence: God's Plan for Humankind

their selves to harmonize with it. There is in Taoism no sense of personal God nor does the Tao exert itself in a personal manner to direct changes in human behavior. It simply exists, immutable and pervasive, for us to discover and accept. One's participation in the Tao, the extent of which determines one's happiness and well-being, is entirely a matter of the choices one makes.

Judaism asserts that the natural world is the creation of God, reflects God's nature, and is the arena in which God constantly acts to reveal the Divine and develop humanity into the image of the Divine. Although the natural world reflects the nature of the Divine, it is not a part of the Divine Who is wholly Other. The relationship between God and his creation, particularly humankind, and most particularly the Jewish people, is covenantal; God covenants with those he selects to be his people to bless and protect them, and they covenant to obey his law and express his will for all humankind. Throughout their history, the Jews believe, God has initiated this relationship and has chosen them for special responsibility. Through the prophets God has given the Law and continues to call people into compliance. The purpose of the chosen people is to be a blessing to all the earth and all earth's people in bringing about the fulfillment of human society, the kingdom of God. Judaism places this kingdom of God firmly in the natural world, although its realization will result in radical transformation of this world into one of complete harmony, peace, and righteousness.

Islam's view of the natural world builds on the same fundamental creation myth as does Judaism and Christianity. The natural world is seen as fully real, the direct and perfect creation of God designed as the venue through which all people pass on their way to eternity. The choices each makes in this life determine their state in the life hereafter. Islam believes that God has laid out the divine requirements for humanity and that judgment will be rendered to each individual as to how fully they surrendered to God's will in this life. While God's chief characteristic toward humankind is mercy and love, human beings are fully responsible for their choices and will receive the fate they deserve. The afterlife in Islam is eternal and divine and dominates

The Natural World

Islamic thought. Islam does not focus on transforming this world into some ideal state but simply accepts it as the proving ground for individual faithfulness and piety. The primary task of the religion is to spread the word of the truth it espouses and help those who have heard its message to remain faithful.

Christianity shares much with the other major world religions. It affirms that the natural world is the direct, intentional, and real creation of God. But it also affirms that it is both temporary and finite and that God is essentially transcendent, eternal, and holy, without bound or division. The material world functions according to natural laws instituted by God, many discoverable by the human intellect. On the other hand, it is wholly dependent on and sustained by God and reflects the divine nature. But it is not part of God, nor is God in any way dependent on it. It is the expression of God's will and provides its creatures with information about God, but access to the Divine is beyond the inherent nature of those in the natural world, except that God initiate and provide that access as a divine gracious act. Christianity also looks for a transformation of the natural world into the kingdom of God, much as in Judaism, but it is divided as to whether this kingdom is earthly or heavenly. Christians do assert that Jesus Christ will come into the natural world bodily at the end of time, but the exact nature of the kingdom he will bring/cause remains controversial.

The young American frontier prophet Joseph Smith Jr. recorded another revelation in 1832 that speaks with mythical, poetic eloquence to the nature of the created universe, particularly its dependence on the spiritual.

> "Wherefore I now send upon you another Comforter... even the Holy Spirit of promise, which other Comforter is the same that I promised unto my disciples, as is recorded in the testimony of John.
>
> This Comforter is the promise which I give unto you of eternal life, even the glory of the celestial kingdom; which glory is that of the church of the

Divine Providence: God's Plan for Humankind

Firstborn, even of God, the holiest of all, through Jesus Christ, his Son;

he that ascended up on high, as also he descended below all things, in that he comprehended all things, that he might be in all and through all things, the light of truth, which truth shineth. This is the light of Christ.

As also he is in the sun, and the light of the sun, and the power thereof by which it was made.

As also he is in the moon, and is the light of the moon, and the power thereof by which it was made.

As also the light of the stars, and the power thereof by which they were made.

And the earth also, and the power thereof, even the earth upon which you stand.

And the light which now shineth, which giveth you light, is through him who enlighteneth your eyes, which is the same light that quickeneth your understandings; which light proceedeth forth from the presence of God, to fill the immensity of space.

The light which is in all things; which giveth life to all things; which is the law by which all things are governed; even the power of God who sitteth upon his throne, who is in the bosom of eternity, who is in the midst of all things.....

And again, verily I say unto you, that which is governed by law, is also preserved by law, and perfected and sanctified by the same.

That which breaketh a law, and abideth not by law, but seeketh to become a law unto itself, and willeth to abide in sin, and altogether abideth in sin, cannot be sanctified by law, neither by mercy, justice, or judgment; therefore, they must remain filthy still.

All kingdoms have a law given; and there are many kingdoms; for there is no space in the which there is no kingdom; and there is no kingdom in which there is no space, either a greater or lesser kingdom.

And unto every kingdom is given a law; and unto every law there are certain bounds also, and conditions.

All beings who abide not in these conditions, are not justified; for intelligence cleaveth unto intelligence; wisdom receiveth wisdom; truth embraceth truth; virtue loveth virtue; light cleaveth unto light;

mercy hath compassion on mercy, and claimeth her own; justice continueth its course, and claimeth its own; judgment goeth before the face of him who sitteth upon the throne, and governeth and executeth all things;

he comprehendeth all things, and all things are before him, and all things are round about him; and he is above all things, and in all things, and is through all things, and is round about all things; and all things are by him, and of him; even God, for ever and ever.

And again, verily I say unto you, He hath given a law unto all things by which they move in their times, and their seasons; and their courses are fixed; even the courses of the heavens, and the earth; which comprehend the earth and all the planets;

and they give light to each other in their times, and in their seasons, in their minutes, in their hours, in their days, in their weeks, in their months, in their years; all these are one year with God, but not with man.

The earth rolls upon her wings; and the sun giveth his light by day, and the moon giveth her light by night; and the stars also giveth their light, as they roll upon their wings, in their glory, in the midst of the power of God.

Unto what shall I liken these kingdoms, that ye may understand?

Divine Providence: God's Plan for Humankind

> Behold, all these are kingdoms, and any man who hath seen any or the least of these, hath seen God moving in his majesty and power.[41]"

Modern science investigates the natural world effectively. Over the centuries philosophers and thinkers have struggled to correlate their observations of natural phenomena with theories of the structure and function of the natural world. The theories are important because they provide a basis for predicting how nature will function in the future. This provides a sense of security and a measure of control. Prior to the development of the modern scientific method, the theories proposed often incorporated theological and/or metaphysical concepts. The underlying assumption of scientific inquiry is that the natural world functions according to laws that always apply. Progress in science is made by the discovery of these laws. The method of correlating observation with the theory has been enhanced in modern science by the use of controlled experiments. This introduces systematic collection of data and the repeatability of results for better correlation of observation and theory. When the data does not support the theory, we must examine the theory and modify or replace it with one able to account for the observed data.

From the scientific perspective, the problem with theological or metaphysical concepts is our inability to run controlled experiments to verify them. Divine realms and beings are "above" this world and its inhabitants and are not readily accessible nor subject to our scrutiny and manipulation. Also, the actors in many theological theories do not necessarily function according to predetermined laws that we know. This unpredictability is the essence of free will, but it leaves scientific investigators with uncertainty about the verification of their concepts. Scientific investigation, unable to handle theological and metaphysical concepts, ignores and often tries to bypass or explain away those concepts in its effort to provide us with control over our envi-

---

[41] Doctrine and Covenants 85:1c-3b; 8-12 (Independence, Missouri: Herald Publishing House, 1978).

The Natural World

ronment and destiny. The theories and hypotheses of science thus exclude metaphysical or theological concepts.

In the emergence of the modern era some of the most prominent conflicts between theological concepts and scientific investigation have been won by science. For example, in the Middle Ages, European astronomers and mathematicians studying the movement of heavenly bodies began to find evidence that the earth was not the center of the observable universe, an idea long assumed by most people. Church leaders tried to suppress such evidence on the basis of interpretations of scripture by earlier church luminaries which placed the earth and humankind as the focus of divine creation. In doing so, church leadership made the mistake of confusing mythical and poetic efforts of the writers of scripture to express spiritual truths in earthly language with scientific, material truth. The insistence by the church that it had all truth and the equal insistence by developing science that it had the key to discovering all truth led to an inevitable impasse between the two.[42] The increasing technological development of telescopes, spectrometers, and computers has continued to reinforce the positions of the scientists until now few doubt their description of the structure of the known universe. The church was increasingly seen by many as archaic and increasingly lacking authority and irrelevant. Only in recent times have some church leaders and theologians attempted to reclaim the scriptural teachings in their mythical and poetic language as spiritual insights rather than literal scientific information. Some fundamentalist groups continue to hold scripture as literal and deny the evidence of science.

Having succeeded in describing much of the current structure of the observable universe, science then attempted to discover how it came into being. This effort has two main branches, geology/paleontology which investigate the structure of the earth and the remains of life forms found; and physics, particularly astro-physics which tries to discover how the universe is changing over time, and nuclear physics which tries to discover the

---

[42] See Armstrong, *The Battle for God*, particularly the Introduction, for a lucid discussion of this phenomenon.

nature and function of physical matter. Both of these fields challenged the church's traditional time-frame involved in the creation and development of the universe and human life. Geology showed that both the earth itself and emerging life forms have vastly longer histories than a literal reading of scripture allows. The failure of church leaders to appreciate the mythical nature of the creation stories created a conflict. Science again won the day and the church's authority was undermined in the minds of many modern people.

As the science of physics developed, Isaac Newton and later, Laplace, hypothesized that the functioning of the entire universe is governed by a comprehensive set of natural laws. Neither Laplace nor Newton, a deeply religious man, ever discounted the action of God as the initial creator and framer of these laws, but they took the view that once the laws were established, the natural world was left to function on its own as a clock-work universe. They believed that humankind was responsible for discovering the laws by which nature functions and learning to control them for our benefit. This assessment of the power of science to discover and control the natural world became the paradigm of modernity. Over the years academics in fields such as sociology, psychology, and history have tried to adapt scientific methodology derived from the physical and biological sciences to their disciplines. Such adaptation has been only partially successful. The scientific method requires experimentation under controlled conditions and repeatable results. Fields dealing with human activity and individual behaviors are seldom able to provide such control and repetition. While many academic fields have benefited from the systematic approach to their studies imposed by their adaptation of scientific methodology, problems arise when practitioners in these disciplines claim more certainty than their data and methodology justifies. Many, particularly academics, have adopted the unscientific view that science is the only way of obtaining knowledge of the world in which we live and, therefore, anything science cannot handle does not actually

The Natural World

exist.[43] The answers to the most fundamental questions of human existence remain unanswerable by science.

At both extremes, the very large and the very small, the natural world remains unknown and unexplained by science. Nuclear physicists pushed their knowledge of the basic structure of matter through atoms to electrons, protons, and neutrons to quarks and smaller particles. It turns out that matter as we experience it in our daily lives is actually energy, which we also experience, but in different ways. Einstein theorized that all existence is energy and that matter is a special case of energy, a packaging of energy in a particular manner. It turns out that when the creation myth has God saying "Let there be light" as the initial creative act, it was expressing in a poetic way a scientific truth as well as a mythical truth. Einstein and others also demonstrated that Newton's laws were not really comprehensive, as other factors and forces are also at play in the universe. These become increasingly important as matter moves at high speed and great distance. The Newtonian theory of mechanics was replaced with Einstein's general theory of relativity, which not only relates matter and energy, but also says that time is relative to the observer, particularly significant at high relative speeds. At high speeds and great distances matter and energy both are seen to act in an "irrational" manner. Light bends, mass increases, time slows down, and space seems to be curved and finite.

A few years ago, British scientist Stephen Hawking wrote a book to share what theoretical physicists think they know about the origin and likely fate of the physical universe in terms that could be understood by normally educated people.[44] He states the issues and the problems of understanding them scientifically as follows: "...where did the universe come from? How and why did it begin? Will it come to an end, and if so, how? These

---

[43] Huston Smith has dubbed this characteristic attitude of modernity *Scientism*, and explores this phenomenon in his books *Forgotten Truth* and *Beyond the Post-Modern Mind*.
[44] Stephen Hawking, *A Brief History of Time* (London: Bantam Books, 1988), ix.

are questions that are of interest to us all. But modern science has become so technical that only a very small number of specialists are able to master the mathematics used to describe them. Yet the basic ideas about the origin and fate of the universe can be stated without mathematics in a form that people without a scientific education can understand."[45] While this implies that these questions can be understood scientifically, he later admits that scientists have reasonable confidence as to *what* happened at the origins of the universe and can make some predictions as to *how* it may end, but have only theories as to *how* it came into being and no idea *why*.

Science theorizes that the universe began with the Big Bang. This theory says that all the matter/energy in the universe was originally concentrated in a point of zero size and infinitely large energy that exploded, sending the matter/energy out in an ever-expanding envelope. This event occurred about fifteen billion years ago.[46] As it expanded, the energy cooled and condensed into particles of matter and, through a series of localized collapses and secondary explosions, formed into galaxies, stars, and planets. The expansion of the universe continues under the initial impetus of the Big Bang, but is gradually slowing[47] due to the mutual gravitational attraction of the matter that has been formed. It is significant that as scientists continue to explore and attempt to confirm this theory, they discover evidence that contradicts the theory itself. The evidence now seems to suggest that in the initial instant [the first trillion-trillionth of a second!] the universe went from zero size to a size larger than all of currently observable space.[48] Such speed for the expansion of light, let alone matter, defies the assumed limit for all movement in the universe, the speed of light. Science has yet no explanation or

---

[45] Hawking. ix.
[46] More recent estimates put it at about 13.7 billion years.
[47] Some data seems to suggest the expansion is accelerating, so controversy continues even within the scientific community.
[48] Reported in the *Hawaii Tribune-Herald*, March 17, 2006. The measurements are scheduled to be published in a future issue of the Astrophysical Journal, according to the report.

even theory to account for this anomaly. Also, if such an initial distribution of matter/energy occurred in the first instant of existence, what slowed it down to its current rate of expansion? Debate continues as to whether the expansion will continue indefinitely or eventually stop and start to contract. If expansion continues, the energy will eventually become so dissipated that all the stars will burn out and matter will become inert and totally cold, the so-called Big Freeze. If gravity wins out, the matter will all collapse into an infinitely dense point with infinite energy again. Then the whole process is likely to start over.

The Big Bang theory, which currently seems to have won the day among scientists, still does not explain the origin of the material universe, even theoretically; it only describes what seems to have happened and projects what will probably continue to happen. The origin of the infinitely dense singularity from which it all began remains unaccounted for. Dr. Hawkings suggests that the original singularity had no energy and that the energy we observe today was the result of this nothingness splitting into energy and anti-energy, matter and anti-matter. While ingenious, such a theory still provides no explanation for the impetus for such an extraordinary development. In his reading of present-day science, time is also finite, having a beginning at the Big Bang and an ending at the final collapse of energy/matter into a single point. This agrees with the theological pronouncements of the creation myth and the prophetic Last Day. In reality, it confirms that science simply has no tools for saying anything about what is real outside of the natural world and, as yet, is even unable to account for what it does describe.

On the other end of the spectrum, as scientists worked with smaller and smaller units of matter, they observed that these particles did not behave in accordance with the laws of physics proven in accordance with Newton's and Einstein's theories. A new theory was needed to encompass the newly acquired data, and quantum mechanics was born. In this area, more irrational behavior is observed. Particles seem to travel two different paths simultaneously; electrons seem to jump from one position to another without traversing the intervening space. Quantum mechanics, however, seems relevant only in the region of extremely small particles/energy packets. It is also employed to describe how matter/energy must have developed in the initial stages of the Big Bang. But how and why the behavior transitions from one mode to the other remains unexplained. Science now has two partial and seemingly contradictory theories: Einstein's general theory of relativity and quantum mechanics. The search for a unified theory continues, but scientists admit they may not have the ability to prove any broader theory, as they are up against limits of energy and observability; they cannot reproduce the conditions of the Big Bang, and some of the processes about which they theorize are changed by the very act of observing or attempting to measure them. Efforts to provide a unified theory continue to occupy scientists, and new concepts such as string theory with its ten dimensions and now membrane theory with its eleven dimensions are being posited and explored. But science remains limited to working to explain *what* happens and *how* natural processes work, but provides no insight as to how the natural world came into being, why the laws of nature are framed as they are, and what it means.

In addition to the field of cosmology, the conflict between religion and science is notably being waged in the field of the development of life on earth. The work of the British scientist Charles Darwin and others created the theory of the evolution of living things. This holds that all living creatures developed gradually from the simplest to the increasingly complex and diverse forms of plants and animals we know today. The theory hypothesizes that this development from lower to higher forms of life occurred as the working of natural law and chance mutations in a process called natural selection. It holds that chance mutations caused by environmental factors occasionally produce characteristics that improve a creature's ability to survive and reproduce. Since reproduction is enhanced for these creatures, the improvement is passed on more readily and the species population of enhanced creatures becomes dominant. This is termed survival of the fittest.

Darwin developed his theory based on his observations in two areas. First, he noted that the life forms he observed on the isolated Galapagos Islands tended to be different from similar forms on the mainland of South America. He speculated that the isolation of the two populations over a long period of time had resulted in their divergent evolution. Secondly, the fossil record found in sedimentary rock formations seemed to support the idea that the earliest life forms were exclusively simple and later life forms more complex and diverse. He theorized that this record supported the idea of complex forms evolving from simpler forms. Darwin's observations of the differences in the life forms in various areas and the fossil record indicate what happened in the past. Darwin's work to this point is what is known as descriptive science, which tells us how things are and, in some cases, what happened in the past. His theory as to the cause of the differences he observed was a hypothesis and is an example of what is called instructional science.[49] In instructional science the intent is to show *how* and *why* the observed phenomena happen. However, unlike many scientific theories, Darwin's evolution hypothesis could not, and can not, be tested. The changes observed took place over vast periods of time and were neither observable nor repeatable in an experimental process. In such cases instructional science is inappropriate. Yet the Darwinian hypothesis, as further developed by others, has passed from hypothesis to established fact in the minds of many. This is because science has been unable to devise a better hypothesis and many modern people are unwilling to admit to non-scientific phenomena in the natural world.[50]

Briefly, the Darwinian hypothesis fails to move from scientific theory to scientifically established fact on the following grounds:

---

[49] See E. F. Schumacher, *Guide for the Perplexed* (New York: Harper & Row, 1976), 100–110 for a fuller explanation of the differences in the two forms of science.

[50] See Smith, *Beyond the Post-Modern Mind*, 161–183 for a more comprehensive criticism of Darwinian evolutional theory.

Divine Providence: God's Plan for Humankind

1. The fossil record does not support the gradual evolutionary changes the theory requires. Darwin himself wrote, "Geology... does not reveal...finely graded organic change... and this, perhaps is the most obvious and gravest objection which can be urged against [my] theory."[51] Darwin's hope that more fossils attesting to the transitional stages between different species and classes of life forms would be found has not occurred to any significant degree, although scientific and popular publications continue to celebrate every new fossilized forms found which seem to have previously unseen characteristics. This lack of evidence for missing links has given rise to the more recent revision to Darwin's theory, punctuated equilibrium. This variant holds that the changes needed to transform life from lower to higher forms occurred in short bursts, possibly caused by rapid environmental changes such as solar flares, comets, or volcanic activity. However, the geological record does not show evidence of such correlated phenomena, with the possible exception of the demise of the dinosaurs, which resulted in destruction of life, not evolution to new forms.

2. The breeding of domestic plants and animals to enhance certain traits has been documented by modern science. However, what it has demonstrated exhaustively is that while changes within species can be induced (micro-evolution), changes from one species to another (macro-evolution) do not occur naturally. Beyond a certain point of deviation from the norm, the changes become unstable and further change is blocked. Luther Burbank noted, "there is a pull toward the mean which keeps all living things within some more or less fixed limitations."[52] Efforts to artificially cross-breed species generally result in sterile offspring.

3. The proposed driver of the theory of natural selection, survival of the fittest, is not supported by the fossil record. Although new, more complex species appear suddenly in the fossil record from time to time, the species from which they suppos-

---

[51] Charles Darwin, *The Origin of Species* (London: J. M. Dent, 1971), 239.
[52] Luther Burbank, quoted in Norman Macbeth, *Darwin Revisited* (Boston: Gambit, 1971), 35.

edly evolved also continue to flourish in many cases. If the fittest survive, why don't the less fit disappear? There are certainly indications of extinctions of life forms, but the timing and rate of decline bears no correlation with the emergence of new forms. Further, the theory of natural selection makes no allowance for the emergence of whole new attributes between supposed ancestors and new species. Species are defined by unique characteristics. Every new trait must be immediately advantageous for natural selection to work. Yet complex organs or limbs require a myriad of changes to become functional. According to natural selection the many changes required to introduce new physical structures occur by random chance over many generations and in more than one individual for the change to be sustained and become dominant. "What good is half a jaw or half a wing?"[53] The uselessness of partially developed organs or appendages would be a disadvantage rather than an advantage in terms of survival and reproduction.

4. The idea of biogenesis, the emergence of life from non-life, which many followers of Darwinism espouse, has yet to be demonstrated under any conditions, let alone those thought to have been the natural environment at the time the first organisms appear in the fossil record. Science has learned to manipulate life in many ways and can readily destroy life, but is unable to create it.

5. One of the tools developed by science is that of statistics. Statistics is a set of mathematical processes by which we are able to predict the probable outcome of random events based on our experience with many such events. While probability is never certainty, because the laws of nature have proven to be highly reliable if we know the conditions under which the random events will take place, we can calculate with great confidence the likely outcome of a large collection of events. When scientists who are skilled in statistics consider the probability of natural selection accounting for the innumerable precise random mutations occurring in the required sequence at the required

---

[53] Stephen Jay Gould, "The Return of Hopeful Monsters," *Natural History* 86, June-July 1977, 24.

time to have resulted in the emergence of the present abundance and diversity of life forms from non-life, or even from simple life, they conclude that there simply has not been enough time in the history of our planet. Some scientists who are aware of this limitation have turned to other possibilities for explaining our present situation, such as life migrating from elsewhere in the universe to earth. There is no evidence for such speculation, but if one hypothesis proves to be untenable, others, no matter how unlikely must be considered. If you limit yourself to science, the challenges of explaining the origin and development of life, particularly human life, are daunting.[54]

The importance of this brief critique of Darwinism is not to debunk or disparage science but rather to place it in its proper context and acknowledge its limitations. Both evolution and astro-physics as descriptive science are impressive and useful, but as instructive science they are untenable. We must look elsewhere for the cause and impetus of the immensely complex universe and life we currently observe.[55]

Inherent in the exploration of the natural world is an age-old philosophical question as well as the scientific one discussed above. That is the question of the apparent contradiction between the nature of the Divine and the nature of the natural world. Philosophers have argued that if the Divine is infinite and holy, without any limitation or division, then any creation by the

---

[54] See Lee Strobel, *The Case for a Creator* (Grand Rapids: Zondervan, 2004), for a readable but well-documented discussion of the current argument between Darwinists and supporters of the various creationist beliefs.

[55] The current political debate about the teaching of evolution in school science classes tends to continue the misuse of both science and religion. Religious people pushing for the introduction of creationism or intelligent design into the science curriculum repeat the fatal error of churchmen during the Enlightenment, confusing myth and history. Scientists continue to repeat the error that science is the only way by which knowledge can be obtained. Evolution should be taught as descriptive science and creationism or intelligent design taught as religion by churches or as literature or anthropology in schools where such curriculum exists.

The Natural World

Divine must also be infinite and holy.[56] The idea seems to be that since in the Divine all possibilities exist, whatever is possible must also be actual. This is a rather curious concept that seems to hinge on the idea that the Divine, being perfect and pervasive, is inherently incapable of creating anything less than perfect or lacking in any way. Thus, any possible configuration of created beings must include all possible configurations. Since in the observable universe not all possibilities are actual, the implication is that the Divine is not yet fully perfect, infinite, and holy, but only relatively so. This implies that God is evolving along with the universe. Such an assertion supports the theory known as process theology. This argument reflects once again the human point of view as opposed to the divinely revealed perspective. If the created universe as we know it is all that exists and the Divine is contained within it, such a perspective might logically be derived. But if, as the great religions assert, the natural world is the creation of the Divine, and the Divine has free will, then the natural world will have whatever character the Divine chooses to give it. This does not preclude other possible configurations for other creations, although we have no information concerning any.

In a mythical or poetic way, Joseph Smith's revelation speaks to these questions. While acknowledging the operation of natural law in every aspect of the natural world, it asserts that God is both the framer of these laws and the power by which they operate. It is significant that the revelation focuses on light as both the fundamental power of the natural world and the symbol of the spirit and intellect that provided meaning and purpose to the natural world. Einstein's work demonstrated the central and limiting nature of light; it appears to be a fundamental constant of the natural world. Because the speed of light is a finite number and is apparently the limit of relative speed, the universe has finite size. The Big Bang theory implies that time also is finite. While both the size and duration of the universe

---

[56] See Arthur O. Lovejoy, *The Great Chain of Being* (Cambridge: Harvard University Press, 1936), for a summary of the historical development of this philosophical position.

are so vast as to be almost incomprehensible to human beings, we are capable of conceptualizing these limits and working with them mathematically. In an earlier vision, Joseph Smith has God speaking to Moses on this subject.

> "And the Lord God spake unto Moses saying, The heavens, they are many and they cannot be numbered unto man, but they are numbered unto me, for they are mine; and as one earth shall pass away, and the heavens thereof, even so shall another come; and there is no end to my work, neither to my words; for this is my work and my glory, to bring to pass the immortality, and eternal life of man."[57]

Whether one thinks of the processes of super novas and black holes within the existing universe or the Big Bang and eventual collapse of the entire universe predicted in some theories, the revelation places the whole context of the natural world in the control of God who is outside of the process. While we cannot comprehend it, we can conceptualize God as being outside of both time and space, causing them to come into existence and presiding over their function for some duration, but more importantly, for some purpose. The mythical and poetical language of the revelation conveys meaning and purpose to us that science can only imply but not demonstrate.[58]

It is significant that a fundamental characteristic of the natural world is opposition. All natural processes seem to be cyclical. Natural structures, minerals, vegetables, and animals grow, mature and stabilize, then began to disintegrate or die. From the time they come into existence, all things are subjected to forces trying to destroy them. Even the diversity of basic physical elements has apparently been built up out of the combining of the simplest atomic forms. While fundamental elements seem to

---

[57] Doctrine and Covenants 22:23.
[58] I do not mean to imply that the only purpose for the created natural world is the development of humanity, but that this purpose is probably the only one humankind can handle.

The Natural World

remain constant in the mature contemporary world we experience, their formation and destruction continue in a long time frame. Land forms are in constant change; mountains are raised or built by volcanic and tectonic forces and immediately are subjected to the actions of wind, water, and temperature change which erode and break them down. While these processes tend to take a long time, they can often be seen and measured. But the life cycles of plants and animals, including human beings, are readily observable. All living forms are in competition for resources needed for growth and health, and all eventually experience decline and death in spite of an abundance of life-sustaining nutrients. Moreover, in the animal world, sustenance for each creature requires the destruction and consumption of other organic entities. In the midst of the competitive, cyclical, natural world, humans sense the eternal, including something at the core that transcends and endures despite the limitations and constant changes of physical, mortal life.

The natural world is awesome in its complexity, beauty, and elegant efficiency. Human beings have always experienced it as marvelously ambiguous; it is both physically and emotionally nurturing and perilous, giving pleasure and pain, comfort and angst. It bespeaks superhuman origins and maintenance, both beneficent and destructive. As the prime evidence of a divine intelligence and power it gives mixed signals as to the nature of the Divine. Is it a good creation gone bad? Has its creator set it in motion and moved on to other concerns? Is it the work of two opposing forces? Is it the result of blind and impersonal chance? Deep within the natural world is Mystery which continues to evoke awe within us all. Our understanding of the divine nature and purpose must address and reconcile this apparent ambiguity of the natural world of which humankind is a part.

The Triune God

The reality of God remains beyond human comprehension, but the idea of a threefold God can be seen to be deeply rational, and to be unequivocally a form of monotheism, of belief in one God.[59]

—Keith Ward

As mentioned earlier, every religion attempts to describe the Divine of which it testifies and on which it depends. The Christian concept of the Trinity has troubled both church leaders and followers throughout the ages. It is an attempt to put into human language a concept that transcends the human. Christianity grew out of Judaism whose central tenet is an affirmation of monotheism, the belief that there is one God and that God is holy, perfect unity. This heritage was challenged by the disciples of Jesus who gradually came to understand that the life, ministry, death and resurrection of Jesus demonstrated that God had become incarnate in their personal experience. For them this was not an abstract theological concept but a living reality. Moreover, they

---

[59] Keith Ward, *God, a Guide for the Perplexed* (Oxford: Oneworld Publications, 2003), 236.

continued to experience the reality of God in the form of the Holy Spirit, the living presence of Christ. For its first three centuries, leaders of the emerging Christian church struggled with the seeming contradiction between the ideas of the unity and absoluteness of God and their testimony of Jesus and the Holy Spirit, with various formulations being espoused by different leaders at different times. Their need to resolve this logical contradiction was heightened by their confrontation with and assimilation of Greek philosophical thought that dominated the culture of the Roman Empire. Finally, at the Council of Nicaea in 325 C.E., an official doctrine for the church was worked out by church leaders. This doctrine was finally articulated in the Nicene Creed by the Council of Constantinople in 381 C.E. It holds that Jesus Christ is fully God and not a creation, adoption, or emanation from God. As an affirmation of a theological principle it is clear, but as an explanation as to how the Divine and human were transposed or combined without either being temporarily lost or without becoming something not fully either, it continues to elicit discussion, argument, and dissension among Christians. The human/divine congruence in Jesus and the unity/contrast of Father, Son, and Spirit were embraced but not explained.

The nature of the Holy Spirit, or Comforter or Paraclete, also posed problems for church leaders. It was also the subject of church councils and was to become the focus of the split between the Eastern Orthodox Church and the Roman Catholic Church. The issue, known as the *Filioque,* is the assertion by the Western church that the Holy Spirit proceeds from the Father *and* from the Son. The Eastern formulation is that the Holy Spirit proceeds from the Father *through* the Son. For Western Christianity, Augustine described the Holy Spirit as being the love between the Father and Son. This formulation seems to have been the one most prevalent in the West through the Middle Ages. However, it does little to support the idea of the Holy Spirit being the third person of the Trinity. As a challenge to perceived abuses of authority by the medieval Roman church, Protestants invoke the Holy Spirit as the authority and power by which all understanding of the divine nature and will is made available to humankind. They affirm that the gospel is contained in the scriptures but the Holy Spirit must give it life and correct interpretation. Although spoken of as the Spirit of God or the Spirit of Christ, in reality most Protestants think of the Holy Spirit as a distinct entity mystically bound to the Father and Son and doing their will in the human arena. For Roman Catholics, the Holy Spirit is more closely associated with the Father and Son. It is also not the only entity available to intercede with them on behalf of humanity, as they also invoke for this purpose Mary, the sinless mother of God, and the saints, human beings who have attained access to God by their righteousness.

The work for which the American prophet Joseph Smith Jr. is best known provides a different understanding of the Trinity. In the Book of Mormon, the prophet Abinadi foretells the incarnation of Jesus:

> "I would that ye should understand that God himself shall come down among the children of men, and shall redeem his people;
>
> And because he dwelleth in flesh, he shall be called the Son of God:
>
> And having subjected the flesh to the will of the Father, being the Father and the Son; the Father because he was conceived by the power of God; and the Son, because of the flesh; thus becoming the Father and Son:
>
> And they are one God, yea, the very eternal Father of heaven and earth."[60]

Earlier, the spiritual leader of the Book of Mormon's Jaredite people records his experience with the pre-existent Christ, of whose existence and nature he was previously unaware. The mythical story tells of a group of people who are dispersed from the Tower of Babel and traveling to a new land. Seeking a

---

[60] Book of Mormon, Mosiah 8:28-31, 1908 Authorized Edition (Independence, Missouri: Herald Publishing House, 1986).

The Triune God

means for lighting the closed ships his people have prepared to cross the ocean, the Brother of Jared prepares sixteen stones and makes an unusual, but full-of-faith request of God.

> "I know, O Lord, that thou hast all power, and can do whatsoever thou wilt for the benefit of man; therefore touch these stones, O Lord, with thy finger, and prepare them that they may shine forth in darkness; and they shall shine forth unto us in the vessels which we have prepared, that we may have light while we shall cross the sea.
>
> Behold, O Lord, thou canst do this. We know that thou art able to shew forth great power, which looks small unto the understanding of men.
>
> And it came to pass that when the Brother of Jared had said these words, behold, the Lord stretched forth his hand and touched the stones, one by one, with his finger;
>
> And the vail was taken from off the eyes of the Brother of Jared, and he saw the finger of the Lord; and it was as the finger of a man, like unto flesh and blood; and the Brother of Jared fell down before the Lord, for he was struck with fear.
>
> And the Lord saw that the Brother of Jared had fallen to the earth; and the Lord said unto him, Arise, why hast thou fallen?
>
> And he saith unto the Lord, I saw the finger of the Lord, and I feared lest he should smite me; for I knew not that the Lord had flesh and blood.
>
> And the Lord said unto him, Because of thy faith thou hast seen that I shall take upon me flesh and blood; and never has man come before me with such exceeding faith as thou hast; for were it not so, ye could not have seen my finger. Sawest thou more than this?
>
> And he answered, Nay, Lord, shew thyself unto me.

> And the Lord said unto him, Believest thou the words which I shall speak?
>
> And he answered, Yea, Lord, I know that thou speakest the truth, for thou art a God of truth, and canst not lie.
>
> And when he had said these words, behold the Lord shewed himself unto him, and said, Because thou knowest these things, ye are redeemed from the fall; therefore ye are brought back into my presence; therefore I shew myself unto you.
>
> Behold, I am he who was prepared from the foundation of the world to redeem my people. Behold, I am Jesus Christ. I am the Father and the Son.
>
> In me shall all mankind have life, and that eternally, even they who shall believe on my name; and they shall become my sons and daughters.
>
> And never have I shewed myself unto man whom I have created, for never has man believed in me as thou hast.
>
> Seest thou that ye are created after mine own image? Yea, even all men were created in the beginning, after mine own image.
>
> Behold this body, which ye now behold, is the body of my spirit; and man have I created after the body of my spirit; and even as I appear unto thee to be in the spirit, will I appear unto my people in the flesh."[61]

The affirmation of the unity of the Father and Son in the Book of Mormon scriptures and the differentiation of the two aspects based on the divine purpose in natural creation is consistent with the testimony of Jesus by the writer of the fourth gospel. Joseph Smith also modified that slightly, emphasizing the providential or purposeful nature of natural creation by God. In the received text the Gospel of John begins:

---

[61] Book of Mormon, Ether 1:66-81.

The Triune God

"In the beginning was the Word, and the Word was with God, and the Word was God."[62]

Joseph Smith's version reads:

"In the beginning was the gospel preached through the Son. And the gospel was the word, and the word was with the Son, and the Son was with God, and the Son was of God."[63]

Bible interpreters have variously interpreted the term "Word" in the received text as being the Son of God, the Holy Spirit, or the mystical Wisdom poetically described in Ecclesiastes and some apocryphal writings. The received text goes on to affirm the creation of the natural world by this Word, who John the Baptist subsequently identifies as Jesus. This reading of the gospel leaves open to interpretation the pre-existence of the Son or the assumption of the function of the mystical Word by the man Jesus. Smith's version makes clear the central role of God the Son in the creation and the nature of divine providence for humankind. All these scriptures point to an unambiguous concept regarding the second person in the Trinity: God the Son is God as expressed in terms of the natural world. God the Father is a way of talking about God in God's essential being which is spiritual and transcendent, eternal and infinite, rather than material which is both temporary and finite.[64] This reading is more akin to the Hindu formulation of the Divine which differentiates between the "Divine without attributes," God in God's essential being which is totally beyond human comprehension, and the "Divine with attributes," God in relationship with humanity.[65]

---

[62] John 1:1 King James Version (KJV).
[63] John 1:1 IV
[64] The use of male terminology for the transcendent God is somewhat unfortunate as most theologians would hold the transcendent Divine to be without gender. But affirming God to be personal is deemed more important than concern for gender neutrality which the English language does not accommodate.
[65] See Smith, *The World's Religions*, 61, 62.

Divine Providence: God's Plan for Humankind

A further differentiation is also indicated by the scriptures: the incarnation of God in the person of Jesus of Nazareth is a further limiting and more temporary assumption of humanness by God the Son as an essential part of divine providence. There is a difference between God the Son in what he terms his spiritual body and in his human body. The Son's spiritual body is immortal, incorruptible, and not subject to the limitations of human flesh and blood. This spiritual body, revealed to the brother of Jared, is what Jesus also revealed to Peter, James and John in his transfiguration as recorded in the three synoptic gospels.[66] The spiritual body is also the form of Jesus' resurrected body and is what the Apostle Paul tries to describe concerning human resurrection in his first epistle to the Corinthian church.[67]

The process of the incarnation of God into human form as related in the gospels can be understood in at least three ways.

1. Those who believe that Jesus became the Son of God by adoption hold that Jesus was fully human, the product of Mary and an unnamed human father, possibly Joseph. This concept holds that the virgin birth doctrine was invented by the followers of Jesus to bolster their claims of his divinity, a not unprecedented practice among religious cults throughout history.

2. Those who accept the gospel accounts as historically accurate have traditionally held that Mary, a virgin, was impregnated by the introduction of a newly created sperm by God the Holy Spirit. This interpretation tends to give Jesus a maternal but not paternal human heritage. The Roman Catholic Church developed the concept of the immaculate conception, the idea that Mary was also without sin [did not share in the sin of Adam and Eve] by some miraculous means, in order to allow Jesus to be wholly sinless. There is no scriptural support for the concept, but rather it is a rational construct devised to answer a perceived doctrinal contradiction.[68]

---

[66] Matthew 17:1–8; Mark 9:1–8; and Luke 9:28–36 IV.
[67] I Corinthians 15:35–54.
[68] In this construction, the Spirit is the Father of the Son, which raises all sorts of issues with the doctrine of the Trinity which I have never seen addressed in the literature.

3. The third possibility is that both the egg and sperm that resulted in the person of Jesus were newly created material by God the Holy Spirit. Thus, Mary served as a surrogate mother and need not have been sinless to allow Jesus to be genetically sinless, that is, not inheriting the sin of Adam and Eve by propagation. Such an interpretation makes Jesus wholly unique with no human heritage, but fully human. This is an equally valid reading of the scriptures with fewer theological complications.

By going to extremes to separate Jesus from the inherited sinfulness of humankind, Christian leaders and thinkers have assumed that sinfulness is genetically transmitted, that the sin of Adam and Eve has been transmitted to all their descendents as a birthright. This assumption that Adam and Eve were historical persons and their actions introduced sin into the created world is a literal reading of the creation myth and another example of the misuse of myth in religion. There is another understanding of the scriptures regarding sin that is made more obvious by the prophetic insights transmitted through Joseph Smith Jr. This understanding does not contradict the received text if the mythical nature of the text is appropriately applied. That understanding is that sin is simply *separation from God*. This idea does nothing to change the reality of sin but does everything to eliminate the guilt associated with the concept of original sin and the desperate condition of humanity most Christian denominations associate with original sin.

With respect to the sinlessness of Jesus, he was sinless because he was not separate from God; he *was* God in the flesh, incarnate by God the Holy Spirit, and every choice he made was in accordance with the will of God. The Apostle Paul tried to express this concept in his second letter to the Corinthian church, speaking of Christ's work of redemption:

> "...God is in Christ, reconciling the world unto himself, not imputing their trespasses unto them; and hath committed unto us the word of reconciliation.

> Now then we are ambassadors for Christ, as though God did beseech you by us; we pray you in Christ's stead, be ye reconciled to God.
>
> For he hath made him to be sin for us, who knew no sin; that we might be made the righteousness of God in him."[69]

Although Christ was sinless, i.e. not separate from God [being God], he took upon himself the temporary condition of separation from the spiritual reality of the essential nature of God by assuming flesh and blood so that human beings could experience relationship with God in the flesh and choose to be reconciled. Jesus' physical death followed by his resurrection in the form of his spiritual body provides the example, the first fruits of the hope for human resurrection and eternal life.

The early church fathers debated the nature of Jesus for several centuries. They believed that it was necessary for Jesus to be both fully human and fully divine in order for him to be the savior of fallen humanity. However, in this alternate understanding of sin and the fall, the divine nature and a human nature are necessary for Jesus, but a human heritage is not. That would only be necessary if one accepts the idea that

- Adam and Eve were historical persons and that the fall of Adam and Eve, with the resulting condition of separation of humankind from God, was the fault of Adam and Eve and resulted in a depravity in all their descendants that could only be erased by the blood sacrifice of a sinless person. This reading posits a problem that occurs only if one commits the error of making the mythical story of our first parents historical. Such attribution of vindictiveness to God has roots more discernable in Greek and Roman conception than Hebrew belief.

- Humankind had to demonstrate their capacity to attain complete sinlessness in the flesh in order to justify their re-entry into the presence of God. Jesus did this, but had to be fully human to qualify as humanity's representative before the throne of

---

[69] 2 Corinthians 5:19-21 IV.

The Triune God

God. This again focuses on the idea of God being estranged from humankind and needing appeasement or proof of worthiness. It also treats humankind as a class rather than individuals and attributes to the whole of humanity the results of the choices and actions of two of their number. Such treatment denies the free will and the essential dignity and worth of each person.

If, on the other hand, God instituted the separation of humankind from the Divine in order for each person to experience real free choice, and if God provides the conditions for each person to choose between continued separation from or reconciliation to the Divine while in this world, the divine presence must be available but not overt. Then Jesus could be fully divine and assume humanness, including dying a mortal death. This does not mean that any human could do what Jesus did; rather, no human could, because no human is capable of functioning as the Divine. The point of Jesus' incarnation and earthly ministry was not to satisfy the requirement of God for a blood sacrifice or to prove that it was possible for a human to live a sinless life, but to provide humankind with the knowledge and experience of the Divine so that they know the option of becoming reconciled to the Divine is available to them. Yet this presence of God among humankind could not be so obvious that none could deny or ignore or doubt. Then human free choice would be preempted. The role of God the Son in the Incarnation was the ultimate gift of God to humankind and demonstrated divine grace toward all people.

In human form, Jesus interacted with a small number of people. He promised his disciples that when he left them he would send them his spirit, the Comforter, to be with them and in them. This was crucial for the development of the Christian church. But the church has tended to teach that the experience of Pentecost marks the advent of the functioning of the Holy Spirit in the world. It is probably true that the disciples of Jesus taught that the Holy Spirit was available to all who accept Jesus as the Christ; this was their experience. But there is ample testimony in the Old Testament and in the experiences of religious people throughout time and the world that the divine presence is available to any who seek it. If we believe that God is the creator and sustainer of all creation and is a just and loving God, and if we believe that experience with the Divine is necessary for human beings to be able to choose whether or not to have a relationship with the Divine, then we must believe that the Divine is available in some form to each person wherever and whenever they experience earthly life. God the Holy Spirit provides this experience. God the Son provides an example, the archetype, of a human fully in harmony with the Divine.

The early Christian councils argued about the nature of the Holy Spirit, mainly in terms of its origin. The question was, "Did it come from the Father or the Son or from both?" They tended to view it as an emanation of some sort. Some scholars identified the Holy Spirit with Wisdom, the intellect of creation that made the natural world lawful and rational. Augustine called the Holy Spirit the common mind of the Father and Son or the love between them. Again, this issue is an attempt to describe the transcendent in human, immanent terms. The Apostle Peter attributed the authority of prophecy to the Holy Spirit.[70] Yet prophecy was a specialized function limited to those few chosen by God as spokesmen to the whole people. A more comprehensive view of God the Holy Spirit is that of the sustainer of the material world and the divine counterpart of the human spirit resident in each person whenever and wherever they experience mortal life.

Middle Eastern religions tended to be priestly in nature, with an elite class between the Divine and the general populace. The priestly function has always been a two-edged sword. It is supposed to be a bridge between the people and God, interpreting the divine will and instructing the people on accessing the divine presence. But too often the priestly class made themselves a barrier, dispensers of divine wisdom and favor according to their own desires and interests, and the exclusive channel through which the people might approach the Divine.

---

[70] II Peter 1:20–21.

The Triune God

While both the prophetic and priestly functions are deeply embedded in Jewish scriptures and tradition, the Jewish people also have a strong sense of personal intimacy in their relationship with God. Their greatest hero, David, is an example of the concept of direct accessibility of the Divine to ordinary people. As a shepherd boy he developed a strong working relationship with God, a relationship that continued throughout his career as soldier and political leader, although he sometimes strayed from God's good graces. This relationship is often expressed in writings attributed to him; the 23rd Psalm is a prime example. Written in first person, it affirms a personal relationship between the individual and God throughout mortal life and carrying over into eternity. Both in their scriptures and in their tradition, the Jewish people have developed an attitude of intimacy with God that allows them to converse and even argue, when they feel burdened or misused because of their faith. This is always done with deep respect and a sense of privilege afforded them out of their covenantal relationship with God.

Practical Christianity developed the sense that Jesus was the intermediary between humans and the transcendent God. This was because Jesus, having experienced humanness, has a better understanding of human weaknesses, needs, and desires. He is our advocate with the Father, who remains the aloof repository of the Holy and ultimate dispenser of justice for human sin. Jesus is the source of divine mercy and the dispenser of grace, unmerited forgiveness for human sinfulness. The Holy Spirit is the divine guide and helper of individuals, whose plight is too removed from God the Father to be worthy of notice. These simplified expressions of the persons of the Christian Trinity are not the way theologians would attempt to describe God but are instead the unexpressed manner in which many Christians relate to God in their daily lives. These views are extensions of human characteristics and society. While affirming the unity of the Trinity, most practicing Christians tend to think of them in hierarchical terms: the Father above the Son and the Spirit serving both, or the Father begetting the Son and the Spirit emanating from them. This hierarchical view, along with the interposition of Mary, the saints and the church between the human and Divine, diminishes the sense of unity and holiness as a fundamental characteristic of the divine nature.

Instead of bringing the Divine down to the human level, it is better to hold to the unity and holiness of the Divine and admit that humans have a limited capacity to encounter it. In this view, the Trinity is not named as God the Father, Jesus as the Son of God, and the Holy Spirit as the mind or love or power of God, but rather as God the Father, God the Son, and God the Holy Spirit. Because human beings have a limited ability to encounter the Divine, our direct experience is most often with God the Holy Spirit. The Holy Spirit carries the sense of both God the Son as the embodiment, or archetype, of the Divine in human terms, and of God the Father as creator and ultimate reality beyond mortal existence. Widespread testimony of encounter with the Holy Spirit affirms that such experience is not limited in time or space nor does it require special conditions to be met for this to occur. Rather, people in all walks of life, in all religions, in many circumstances claim encounter with a presence from outside themselves impinging on the core of their being in either subtle or dramatic ways, bringing comfort, insight, assurance, and guidance for them personally. In our humanness we experience the larger aspects of the Divine only dimly, and it is in this sense that we say the Holy Spirit testifies of the Father and the Son. Although scripture and history record a few incidents of individuals who under special circumstances have experienced God in bodily form, either in vision or possibly in a transfigured state, divine encounter in bodily form is with God the Son. God the Father, the ultimate reality of the Divine, remains beyond human experience in the natural world yet is the ideal and focus of all true faith and hope. Christians pray to the Father in the name of the Son and by the light or power of the Holy Spirit. Thus we express our vision of that which we dimly see and vaguely comprehend, but this reality is vouchsafed to us by the Divine itself as the Holy Spirit.

The Christian formulation of the Divine, while a true outgrowth of the experiences of a people through the centuries, is flawed in at least one important sense: it adopts the gender bias of the culture in which it arose. While there is no denying that the central expression of the Divine in Christian experience, the Incarnation of God, was in the person of a man, Jesus of Nazareth, and, the record of Jesus' teaching and activity has Jesus referring to the transcendent God as Father, the essential teachings of Jesus and those who preserved and interpreted them make clear the equality of men and women in relationship to the Divine. The creation myth of Christianity affirms that both male and female humanity were created in the image of God. Yet this affirmation does not make gender a characteristic of the transcendent God but only a characteristic of the manifest God in the created world. The problem, of course, is the conflict between asserting the personal nature of the Divine as opposed to asserting the gender of the Divine, since in human experience persons have gender. Some modern theologians and writers have rightly decried the practical effect of the gender bias in Christianity and other religions as a source of suppression of women and denial of their equality both in human culture and before God. Part of their efforts to redress this problem has focused on seeking female images of the Divine in the traditions and/or seeking to develop a new conception of the Divine with female characteristics.

Unfortunately, Christian tradition does not provide many female images for the Divine. In their effort to find them, some writers go back to parts of the Jewish tradition, which Christians have adopted and reinterpreted in the light of the witness of Jesus and the Holy Spirit. These scholars point to the personification of Wisdom in the Old Testament book of Proverbs and the inter-Testament books of Sirach and the Wisdom of Solomon in which this divine trait is given female gender. The term "wisdom" in Greek is *sophia,* which is a feminine noun. Some modern writers have further personified this divine characteristic by capitalizing the term, making it Sophia and asserting it can be substituted for "the Word" of the Gospel of John, the ordering and forming power of divine creation. Jewish tradition has tended to identify Sophia with the Torah, the Books of the Law in which is found all divine wisdom. Some modern Christian feminist writers have tried to identify Sophia with Jesus on the grounds that Jesus embodied divine wisdom. While such images may be helpful to people who feel a need for feminine images of the Divine, it must be remembered that all such images have to do with divine manifestation and not the Divine itself.[71] Focusing on the teaching and actions of Jesus and upholding the worth of all persons are of more value in correcting the gender bias in Christianity. Rather than introducing a Mother God, creating a feminine counterpart to Jesus or depersonalizing Deity, Christians will be better served by focusing on spiritual development that transcends gender.

It is interesting to note that the development of doctrine concerning Mary, the earthly mother of Jesus, within the Roman Catholic tradition, while probably not intended to address the issue of gender bias, had this effect. By the elevation of Mary to the status of primary intercessor for human beings with Christ, by asserting her to be the sinless mother of God, the church provided a powerful female image for worship. Other female saints also serve this function for those needing a less exalted means of access to the Divine than the images of the Trinitarian Divinity who became increasingly remote in Catholic praxis through the centuries. Finding no support for such doctrines in the Bible, Protestants tended to dismiss the glorification of Mary and the saints as proof of the apostasy of the Catholic Church, justifying their break from that faith tradition. As a result, Protestantism has struggled to find equality of genders in doctrine and praxis.

The concept of the Triune God in Christianity has been the focus of much criticism of the religion by others. Yet it makes explicit what other faiths have often accepted and practiced uncritically: developing a relationship with the Divine requires images with which people can identify. The experience of the Divine in the natural world is undeniable in every faith tradition. By recognizing the manifest nature of God the Son and God the

---

[71] See Elizabeth A. Johnson, *She Who Is* (New York: The Crossroad Publishing Company, 1992) for a scholarly and helpful treatment of the efforts to redress the gender bias of traditional Christianity.

The Triune God

Holy Spirit, both the reality and the accessibility of the transcendent God the Father is possible and effective.

The Human Condition

When I consider thy heavens, the work of thy fingers,
the moon and the stars, which thou has ordained;
What is man, that thou art mindful of him?
and the son of man that thou visitest him?
For thou hast made him a little lower than the angels,
and hast crowned him with glory and honour.
Thou madest him to have dominion over the works of thy hands;
thou hast put all things under his feet.
—Psalm 8:3-6

This familiar psalm affirms the place of humanity in the natural world as first expressed in the creation myth of Judaism and Christianity—a created being, not yet fitted for heaven, but with dominance over and responsibility for the rest of the created world. There is also here the promise of a glorious and honorable destiny. However, the reality of human existence in the created world, while conforming to this generic pattern in the aggregate, is more complex and less certain in the specific. Individual people have little control over the natural world and are always subject to the will of other people and the prevailing structures of the society in which they find themselves. Each of us is born into this world totally dependent on other persons; we

The Human Condition

are endowed with limited innate abilities; and we grow up subject to a societal situation not of our own choosing or making over which we can exert limited influence and control. As we gain maturity, our ability to shape our own destiny increases. But regardless of the degree of freedom we are able to realize within the limits of our natural abilities and the nurturing of our families, teachers, and mentors, our choices remain circumscribed, our dominion limited, and our personal achievements ephemeral. For the individual the promise of fulfillment of our potential lies beyond the confined scope and brief span of our earthly life.

One of the great world religions, Buddhism, was founded in reaction to the realization by its founder, Siddhartha Gautama, that human life is fundamentally characterized by suffering, disease, decrepitude, and death.[72] The Christian apostle Paul agrees that human life is subject to bodily corruption and mortality.[73] Religion exists to help people overcome the apparent inevitability and finality of these facts. We look to a life beyond our life in this natural world for fulfillment of the human potential. In fact, all the great world religions, with the possible exception of Confucianism, place the fulfillment of human potential beyond the mortal sphere. And even Confucianism views the state of the ancestors, those who have passed on, as more blessed and honorable than that achievable in mortal life.

Eastern religions have tended to respond to the limitations of time and resources imposed on individuals by the human lifespan by positing a continuing cycle of physical rebirths or reincarnations to which each individual is doomed until they finally "get it right." Getting it right, however, in Hinduism and Buddhism means not reaching fulfillment of human potential in terms of gaining complete dominion in this world, but instead, escaping from this plane of existence altogether. There is in Hinduism no sense of corporate fulfillment, no kingdom of God. While it does advocate for the fulfillment of familial and social responsibilities, it does so for the personal growth such activities

---

[72] Smith, *The World's Religions*, 82–84.
[73] See 1 Corinthians 15.

imply. Its methods focus on the ultimate personal renunciation of all attachments to the material, social, political, and economic factors that are the arena for dominion as we normally understand it. Moreover, the initiative for learning what is required to achieve release from mortal existence lies firmly with each individual being. We may help each other, guide and encourage each other, but each self must ultimately learn to choose between what is eternal within oneself and what is merely temporary and ultimately unreal.

Christianity and Islam have no tradition hinting at reincarnation but have tended to focus on the promise of salvation which is usually understood as being a glorious and joyful existence after mortal life. Such salvation is a gift of God and is dependent on God's judgment on each person's performance in life. Salvation is assured by compliance in this life with the laws and commandments which each faith has set out in their scriptures. Both faiths recognize the limitations and difficulties of mortal life but tend to hold these to be more than compensated for by the wonders and joys of the after-life. The requirements for salvation, however, are a matter of interpretation and have been the cause of fierce debate and rivalry among the various factions of each religion, and between the various religions over the centuries. Both faiths care about this life both in terms of fairness and justice and as a measure of faithfulness, but both look beyond this life for personal fulfillment of our created potential.

Judaism has tended to focus less on the afterlife, although it does not exclude this possibility. With the exception of the mystical development of the middle ages,[74] Judaism has tended toward a pragmatic approach to religion; one should focus on this life and the life to come will take care of itself. In its history, Judaism has consistently looked to the fulfillment of human potential in an earthly, sometimes eschatological future. The idea of a glorious and peaceable kingdom brought about by the leadership of the Messiah pervades Jewish scripture and tradition. While it may require divinely initiated change, the nature of this kingdom

---

[74] See Ben Zion Bokser, *The Jewish Mystical Tradition* (Northvale, New Jersey: Jason Aronson Inc., 1993), for an exploration of this movement.

The Human Condition

is earthly in its pleasures and fulfillments. A final spiritual existence is posited in Jewish writing, but its nature and importance in the practice of Judaism is less than in most of the other world's religions.[75]

Judaism and Christianity have each developed a strong tradition of collective responsibility and fulfillment in addition to addressing individual destiny. The ideal of the kingdom of God on earth focuses on the development of a righteous society in which each individual has their proper place, makes a contribution, and reaps the rewards of peace, security, prosperity, and fulfillment. It is a concept that recognizes the diversity of individual natures and circumstances and endeavors to organize, coordinate, and utilize the gifts of each for the benefit of all. In all religions, individual morality is judged to a large degree by how people treat each other. But Judaism in particular, and Christianity to a lesser degree, hold that the collective society is also subject to moral judgment. Conversely, the possibility of personal righteousness, happiness, and fulfillment is somewhat dependent on the development of righteous society.

There is a strong strain within Judaism, Christianity and Islam often termed piety/prosperity. This concept states that when people are sufficiently pious, when they respect and follow the laws of God, God in turn blesses them with prosperity in the sense of shalom or overall well-being. The focus is very much this-worldly, and all three religions, in a pervasive manner, use this criterion to judge piety. That is, when things go badly for people, it is judgment on their lack of piety. The Jewish scriptures, as well as those of Christianity and Islam, have many references which can easily be interpreted in this vein. It can be noted that this interpretation accords with that of most primitive and tribal religions, and with the Greek heritage which has affected all three of the major religions. When you please God (or the gods), they bless and favor you. Vice-versa, when you displease them, beware of their wrath.

---

[75] Simcha Paull Raphael, *Jewish Views of the Afterlife* (Northvale, New Jersey: Jason Aronson, Inc., 1994).

Divine Providence: God's Plan for Humankind

The problem with the piety/prosperity concept is that we often observe contradictions; bad things happen to good people and the wicked seem to prosper. Religious leaders throughout the ages have attempted to justify such occurrences in a number of ways. Often it is asserted that the trials of good people are sent as a testing of their faith and faithfulness. The Book of Job in the Jewish scriptures is a classic example of this idea. The story is an elaborate parable but is faithful to real-life attitudes and rationalizations. The idea is that having endured the test, the reward of one's faithfulness is that much the greater. Yet in this story Job may receive justice in the end, but what of the innocent lives of his children who are sacrificed unjustly to cause him grief? In life our trials often come at the expense of real harm to apparently innocent victims. If their suffering is caused to inflict pain on us, where is their justice? The answer is that in this world, there is no guarantee of justice. It remains an ideal, a noble goal for human striving, and a standard by which human beings may judge themselves. But the reality of justice remains unrealized for many people in this life.

Another explanation is that our reward for injustices in this life will come in the after- life; we will be rewarded in heaven for our unjust suffering on earth. Likewise, the wicked are doomed to horrible and prolonged suffering after death. This may be true, but it does nothing to bolster the piety/prosperity theory which is focused on justice in this world. Rather, it seems to support the suspicion of many modern people that God has lost control of his creation: God is either not involved in earthly life or else is powerless to prevent injustices here. That God's plan is so easily thwarted by human actions implies a weakness in the divine plan, and thus in the Divine itself that is troubling to many. An arbitrary and ambiguous set of punishments and rewards in the hereafter seems to make this life meaningless. This is unacceptable ethics for many and implies that our own actions are less important and determinant than justice would seem to require.

The human condition is precarious and filled with ambiguity. Mortal life is limited in duration and in scope. The natural world is wonderful and terrible, full of beauty and ugliness, always more than we can comprehend but capable of providing inspiration and scope for dreaming and experiencing real achievement and satisfaction within our limited natures. Within the confines of human limitations there is scope for the realization of meaning and purpose, but for many, this remains a dream. However, humans have the capacity to look beyond our personal limitations, to consider past and future, to remember and to speculate. These capacities cause us to seek meaning and purpose beyond the limitations of our mortal life. Throughout history, people have sought for meaning and purpose in a divine realm of greater being, power, and permanence. The existence of such a realm and such divine beings was not just a way of dealing with the limitations and ambiguities of human existence, but also the response of something deep within the individual human being to a call from this realm. While we project the existence of such divine realms, there is no certainty that the ills and imbalances of human life will be redressed there. The intimations of the prophets and mystics, those who have experienced a glimpse of the divine realm, is not that human affairs are set right, but that human ills and distortions are of little consequence to those who leave this world behind. This assertion is not the same as saying that human actions have no consequence relative to the divine realm. To the contrary, human choices in this life are believed to determine life beyond the mortal world. But the conditions of mortal life have no resolution beyond time and space.

Throughout history, human beings have created a wide variety of cultures and subcultures encompassing family units, villages, tribes, nations, and civilizations. Each entity exemplifies human creativity, perseverance, compassion, ambition—all the possibilities within human nature expressed in variations of organizations and groupings. Although many species exhibit group organization and behavior, humans to a far greater degree have learned to organize themselves into complex social structures intended to improve the wellbeing of the entire group. Often such organization has served to sustain the group, but it has also often led to the exploitation of some by others. Much that is no-

Divine Providence: God's Plan for Humankind

ble and beneficent has been created, but much that is base and repressive has also come about. Human societies are reflective of the ambiguity found within each individual being. The opposition built into the created world is pervasive in all human endeavors as well. In spite of humankind's optimistic expectation of being able to organize itself into an enlightened and beneficent society, no civilization has been able to overcome the baser instincts of some of its members to take advantage of others for their own gain.[76]

Recognizing the human condition is essential for understanding the divine plan for humankind. Any divine plan must be applicable to all persons at all times. The idea fostered by some within every religion that God only cares for those who accept their vision and interpretation, and that all others are sadly lost, is arguably the greatest heresy within every religious tradition. The fundamental premise of any faith that claims their God or Ultimate Reality as the principle behind the natural world must be the universality of the divine plan for humankind. The Eastern religions that believe in reincarnation take care of this issue by simply asserting that everyone keeps being reborn until they are born into a situation where they embrace the true path to escape from the process. For them the divine in the Divine Essence is not personal but an organizing principle for the natural world of which humanity is one entity. Their tradition does not attempt to explain the origin of all that exists but just accepts that somehow it does. In their understanding, existence is a cosmic conveyor belt on which beings are somehow generated as simple life forms, progress through stages of life, finally become people, and eventually pass out of this existence altogether. Their faith is not primarily about meaning and purpose but about process.

The revealed religions begin with a personal God who chooses to communicate with humanity. It is axiomatic that the vision of any prophet is partial but that the vision affirms two important concepts: first that there is a Divine Being and, second

---

[76] See Chapter 6, "Hope Yes: Progress, No" in Smith, *Forgotten Truth*, for a fuller discussion of this evaluation of the human condition.

The Human Condition

that this Divine Being wishes to communicate with humankind. These concepts hold the hope and promise of further communication. Over time, the accumulation of communicated visions provides a framework for a relationship between the human and Divine. The interpretation of the visions provides the basis for religion as faith and praxis. But what happens far too often is that the leaders of the religion forget that the vision impelling the faith is partial and the interpretation necessarily open to revision in the light of additional visions and changing human conditions. Then the religion becomes static and confining instead of living and freeing. When people find meaning, hope, and a sense of purpose in their religious faith, both the religion and the people prosper spiritually, humanly. When people fail to find such meaning, hope, and sense of purpose, they turn from their faith to seek these essential aspects of human existence elsewhere. In spite of the advances in communication, transportation, and other developments of science and technology that characterize the modern/post-modern era—and in some sense, because of them—humanity is no closer to human fulfillment than it has ever been. The answer lies elsewhere, deep within and far beyond the wondrous creature that is the human being.

Revelation and Inspiration

I never spoke with God, nor visited in heaven;
yet certain am I of the spot as if the chart were given.[77]
—Emily Dickinson

    The three great Western religions (Judaism, Christianity, and Islam) all came into being as the result of divine intervention into human affairs. Abraham, the primary patriarch of Judaism, and Moses, its primary prophet and law-giver, embarked upon their careers in response to specific calls and commissions from God. Jesus is held by Christians to be the ultimate revelation of God, God incarnate, stepping into the midst of humanity to reconcile the Divine and human for all time. The Holy Qu'ran, considered to be the very words of God by Muslims, was given through the Prophet Mohammad in a series of encounters with the angel Gabriel who spoke directly for Allah. While the process involved in the founding of the three great Western religions differed in their particulars, all three resulted from the Divine taking the initiative to reveal itself to humanity. They were each constituted in unique historical circumstances which determined

---

[77] *A Treasury of the World's Best Loved Poems*, 164.

Revelation and Inspiration

the framework and context by which they are expressed even today.

While there is no standard in this regard, it is helpful to differentiate between revelation and inspiration. Both involve encounter between the Divine and human, but it helps to think of revelation as being initiated by the Divine and inspiration as being initiated by humans. Often, it may be difficult to determine who initiates the encounter when both seem to be reaching out to the other. However, inspiration tends to address issues with which the person is already engaged, and revelation tends to evoke new insight that results in the human becoming aware of something they had never before considered. Revelation is often thought of as divine disclosure, the sharing by the Divine of something about itself that otherwise would remain hidden from human view. The primary revelations of the great Western religions also involved the disclosure of the divine program for the people to whom the prophet is spokesperson. These programs, or divine providence, always focus on bringing the Divine and human into closer relationship, alignment, and harmony. The inspiration which resulted in the development of the great Eastern religions was also focused on the same divine providence, bringing the Divine and human together.

Religious programs worldwide have many common elements, including worship, prayer, meditation, study, service, and social and moral responsibility. All have as their primary purpose the development of an increasing alignment of the human with the Divine. Religions also acknowledge that both human effort, or at least conscious openness, and Divine support, or grace or inspiration, are needed for progress to be made in this development. Revelation opens to humankind something of the Divine nature and plan, and inspiration provides the necessary guidance, support, and motivation along the way.

Inspiration is often cited as the key to much of what is good and useful in human society, although people may debate as to whether inspiration comes from outside the individual or from some unconscious or subconscious part of the human mind. While acknowledging that the human mind is not yet fully ex-

Divine Providence: God's Plan for Humankind

plored or explained by modern science, many people testify of a sense of encounter with intelligence other than their own when experiencing what they call inspiration. In the same manner that people in many settings sense the existence of a greater power which they call the Divine, people experiencing inspiration sense a personal awareness of another intelligence interacting with their own. Sometimes there is simply a moment of clarity in which the solution to a problem is resolved, but sometimes the encounter evokes a sense of wonder at the experience itself, and we experience the opening of a new vista.

From Judaism, the story of Moses' initial encounter with God is typical of the revelatory experience.

> "Now Moses kept the flock of Jethro his father in law, the priest of Midian: and he led the flock to the backside of the desert, and came to the mountain of God, even to Horeb.
>
> And the angel of the Lord[78] appeared unto him in a flame of fire out of the midst of a bush: and he looked, and, behold, the bush burned with fire, and the bush was not consumed.
>
> And Moses said, I will now turn aside, and see this great sight, why the bush is not burnt.
>
> And when the Lord saw that he turned aside to see, God called unto him out of the midst of the bush, and said, Moses, Moses. And he said, Here am I.
>
> And he said, Draw not nigh hither: put off thy shoes from off thy feet, for the place whereon thou standest is holy ground.
>
> Moreover he said, I am the God of thy father, the God of Abraham, the God of Isaac, and the God of Jacob. And Moses hid his face; for he was afraid to look upon God."[79]

---

[78] Joseph Smith's version changes the angel of the Lord to the presence of the Lord.
[79] Exodus 3:1-6 KJV.

Revelation and Inspiration

Several aspects of this story are significant:

1. God initiated the experience in the midst of Moses' ordinary life.

2. God attracted Moses' attention by creating an unnatural event. This act proclaimed intervention of the Divine unto the mundane world.

3. God called Moses by name and warned him how to behave in the presence of the Divine.

4. God identified himself, establishing personal contact and authority.

Upon making contact, God commissions Moses to return to Egypt to bring the Hebrews out of slavery to the land that is to become Israel. The exchange between God and Moses is almost a negotiation, but in the end, Moses is convinced of God's program and agrees to act as God instructs. Moses has embarked on a career as prophet and spiritual leader for the twelve families descended from the patriarch Jacob, or Israel, as he was named by God when God reaffirmed his covenant with him and his descendants.[80] In this account, God is revealed as a tribal deity concerned only with helping the children of Israel escape the powerful Egyptians and eventually defeat the Canaanites to establish the nation of Israel.

In June 1830, Joseph Smith Jr. recorded a revelation concerning a spiritual encounter between God and Moses in which God revealed to Moses the creation of the natural world and something of God's plan for it. Joseph's retelling of Moses' encounter with God and his commission to bring the children of Israel out of bondage is put into a universal context but is distinctly Christian.

> "The words of God which he spake unto Moses, at a time when Moses was caught up into an exceeding high mountain, and he saw God face to face, and he talked with him, and the glory of God was upon Moses; therefore, Moses could endure his presence.

---

[80] Genesis 35:10–12 IV.

And God spake unto Moses, saying, Behold, I am the Lord God Almighty, and Endless is my name, for I am without beginning of days or end of years; and is not this endless?

And behold, thou art my son, wherefore look, and I will show thee the workmanship of mine hands, but not all;

for my works are without end, and also my words, for they never cease;

wherefore, no man can behold all my works except he behold all my glory;

and no man can behold all my glory, and afterward remain in the flesh, on the earth.

And I have a work for thee, Moses, my son; and thou art in the similitude of mine Only Begotten; and my Only Begotten is and shall be the Savior, for he is full of grace and truth;

but there is no God beside me; and all things are present with me, for I know them all.

And now, behold, this one thing I show unto thee, Moses, my son; for thou art in the world, and now I show it unto thee.

And it came to pass, that Moses looked and beheld the world upon which he was created.

And as Moses beheld the world, and the ends thereof, and all the children of men, which are and which were created; of the same he greatly marveled, and wondered.

And the presence of God withdrew from Moses, that his glory was not upon Moses; and Moses was left unto himself; and as he was left unto himself, he fell unto the earth.

And it came to pass, that it was for the space of many hours before Moses did again receive his natural strength like unto a man; and he said unto himself,

> Now, for this cause, I know that man is nothing, which thing I never had supposed; but now mine eyes have beheld God; but not mine natural but my spiritual eyes, for mine natural eyes could not have beheld, for I should have withered and died in his presence;
>
> but his glory was upon me, and I beheld his face, for I was transfigured before him."[81]

This vision is an exploration in mythical or poetic form of new perspectives on divine revelation, the nature of the created world, the relation between the Divine and human, and God's program for humankind. The vision describes a confrontation between Moses and Satan which Moses wins by invoking the name of the Only Begotten. Then Moses enters a second time into the presence of God, receives his commission to deliver Israel from bondage, and again sees the entire earth and all its inhabitants. Moses asks God the purpose of creation to which God replies,

"The heavens, they are many and they cannot be numbered unto man, but they are numbered unto me, for they are mine; and as one earth shall pass away, and the heavens thereof, even so shall another come; and there is no end to my works, neither to my words; for this is my work and my glory, to bring to pass the immortality, and eternal life of man."[82]

Although modern scholars may try to analyze writings such as this in an effort to determine the validity of the experience or

---

[81] Doctrine and Covenants 22:1-7. I do not suggest that Smith thought that this version of Moses' calling by God should replace the received text. Smith later did rework the King James Bible but did not change the burning bush story. Apparently Smith did not initially know what to do with this vision. It seems to have come independently of anything he was working on at this time. Later in the year [1830] Smith received additional revelations that seem to follow this vision. The later revelations became the revised and elaborated creation myth discussed in an earlier section. This vision was never presented as a part of that myth but was published separately and was later included as a preface to the "Inspired Version" of the Bible published by Smith's son in 1865.

[82] Doctrine and Covenants 22:23.

the likelihood that Smith (or any other person claiming prophetic insight) simply made it up or suffered from some mental disorder, the tools of scientific enquiry are inadequate for such a purpose. Smith was alone when he had the vision (as was Moses when he encountered the burning bush) and he is not available for cross-examination. He left little information concerning the context of the experience nor do we have any record that he ever reflected or commented on the process. The record of a revelatory or inspirational experience must stand on its own merits. If the record speaks to the heart and mind, provides some clarity to human understanding, reaffirms some deeply felt but unarticulated vision, then it serves its purpose. Only such authentic visions survive and help shape human culture and civilization.

One other aspect of revelation and inspiration needs to be considered. People in every culture tend to focus on the person involved in the experience, the prophet, seer, or mystic. Such persons are often held to be special, worthy of admiration or devotion. Yet we often know little about them. For example, as far as we know, the Biblical prophet Amos lived a normal life as a herdsman until God called him to speak to the nation in warning, reproof, and consolation. We can only presume that following this powerful pronouncement he returned to his ordinary life. Others such as Isaiah, Jeremiah, or Ezekiel, seem to have made a career of being a prophet. Yet we know little of them as persons. The essence of the prophetic experience is not the prophet, but the activity of God in reaching out to the people through them. Revelation and prophecy express the free will of God in effecting the development of a group of people and calling them into relationship with the Divine. Certain people may have a propensity to relate to the Divine more easily than others, but it is God's initiative that causes revelation to happen. Speaking for God is never easy and exacts a price on the person involved. Some like Jonah resist mightily, and some may never submit to the call of God to speak. Some who speak prophetically may not fully understand or appreciate the significance of the message they bring. The person involved may or may not embrace the message. The point is that God does not take away

Revelation and Inspiration

the prophet's free will nor relieve the prophet of their responsibility for deciding their course in life. Certainly the prophetic experience can become a significant part of a person's life, but it is not necessarily determinate even for the one through whom God's message is delivered.

Some who claim to speak for God do not express the divine will or purpose. Whether such persons are deluded themselves or are intentionally attempting to delude others, false prophecy or expressions of divine inspiration are a constant danger for human society. Traditions in which people rely on signs from God to guide their actions have abounded throughout history. In Israel and Judah as recorded in Jewish scriptures, the battle between true and false prophets was ongoing. Some people earned their living as prophets advising the king of God's requirements and intentions. Often what they told the king determined their status and material well-being. Such a situation fosters divided loyalty: who is the prophet serving, God or the king? True prophets serve God whether the message they bring is to the liking of the king or not.

Jeremiah is honored in Judaism for speaking God's word faithfully even when it foreshadowed the destruction of the kingdom of Judah and the Babylonian captivity of the Jewish people. In spite of being persecuted and imprisoned for speaking God's truth against the policies of the king and those prophets predicting Judah's victory, Jeremiah persisted. He spoke powerfully the words God gave him.

> "Thus saith the Lord of hosts, Hearken not unto the words of the prophets that prophesy unto you; they make you vain; they speak a vision of their own heart, and not out of the mouth of the Lord.
>
> They say still unto them that despise me, The Lord hath said, Ye shall have peace; and they say unto everyone that walketh after the imagination of his own heart, No evil shall come upon you.

> For who hath stood in the counsel of the Lord, and hath perceived, and heard his word? who hath marked his word and heard it?...
>
> I have not sent these prophets, yet they ran; I have not spoken to them, yet they prophesied.
>
> But if they had stood in my counsel, and had caused my people to hear my words, then they should have turned them from their evil ways, and from the evil of their doing.
>
> Am I a God at hand, saith the Lord, and not a God afar off?
>
> Can any hide himself in secret places that I shall not see him? saith the Lord. Do not I fill heaven and earth? saith the Lord.
>
> I have heard what the prophets said, that prophesied lies in my name, saying, I have dreamed, I have dreamed.
>
> How long shall this be in the hearts of the prophets that prophesy lies? yea, they are prophets of the deceit of their own heart;
>
> Which think to cause my people to forget my name by their dreams, which they tell every man to his neighbor, as their fathers have forgotten my name for Baal.
>
> The prophet that hath a dream, let him tell a dream; and he that hath my word, let him speak my word faithfully."[83]

Inspiration, however, tends to be life-shaping for the person involved. This is because inspiration tends to come as a result of the individual's effort to be guided by the Divine. Inspiration is initiated by the person and is the gift of God in response to human endeavor. This does not ensure that a person accepts the insight they receive; if we do not like the answer to our prayer we are free to ignore or reject it. But generally, when we find an

---

[83] Jeremiah 23:16-18, 21-28.

Revelation and Inspiration

answer we are seeking, we are ready to accept its implications and commit to it. Revelation and inspiration are God's contribution to the struggle by humankind to comprehend the Divine/human equation. They are primarily intellectual but often elicit emotional and functional responses as well. They are expressions of God's grace which draw us upward.

Sin and Salvation

The winds of God's grace are always blowing; it is for us to raise our sails.[84]

—Attributed to Ramakrishna

In all the great religions salvation consists of being in the presence of the Divine in some form. Sin consists of being separated from the Divine, either because the Divine is inaccessible, humans have been cast out of the divine presence, or simply because humans have not yet discovered the divine existence. Each person in the natural world moves toward or away from the Divine by the choices they make. Movements away from the Divine are acts of sin, while movements toward the Divine are acts of righteousness. *Failing* to move toward the Divine is referred to as sin of omission. Whether these choices are unknowing or intentional, the ultimate effect is the same. Only by making choices that align the human will with the divine will can the individual gain awareness of the Divine and find the fulfillment of their potential.

---

[84] Quoted in Novak, *The World's Wisdom*, 41.

Sin and Salvation

Within Christianity, the debate regarding sin and salvation has focused on the degree and manner by which the individual human can determine their own salvation. The Roman Catholic Church has emphasized the authority of the church to mediate salvation through its ordinances; people must choose to submit themselves to the authority of the church. The church believes it has been given this role by God and seeks to be faithful to its responsibility. The Protestant movement has made salvation the direct responsibility of the individual; people must make a personal commitment to Jesus Christ. But the manner in which divine grace effects salvation is understood in various ways. Some within Protestantism hold that God has predestined some humans to be saved and some not, while others hold that salvation is free to all who claim it. In both cases, the grace of God toward humankind is an essential factor; that is, no human can earn their way into heaven by their own efforts.

In the practice of many denominations, sin consists of failing to follow the standards that have been established by divine decree. These standards have been drawn from the interpretation of scripture by church authorities. Christians claim to be following the example of Jesus: the Christian gospels record Jesus interpreting Jewish law and condemning religious leaders for focusing on legalistic rigor rather than the fundamental aspects of love, justice, and mercy. Jewish law is based on the divine pronouncement known as the Ten Commandments, laws given directly to Moses by God on Mount Sinai during the Jewish exodus from Egyptian captivity. Jewish scholars and teachers subsequently derived more than six hundred laws governing human behavior from these basic ten and the ritual instructions in the Torah. At one point, Jesus reportedly condensed all the law and teachings of the prophets into two commandments: love of God and love of neighbor.[85] Still, Christian churches have defined human behavior relative to sin and salvation in terms of obedience to their interpretation of laws derived from scripture. The Roman Catholic Church instituted the sacrament of penance

---

[85] Mark 12:33–36 IV.

consisting of confession of sins coupled with priestly forgiveness and prescribed atonement as necessary for salvation. Protestants have left confession and repentance to the individual but still hold certain behaviors to be fatal to salvation.

Another way of interpreting religious laws is to view them as divine instructions for the development of human spirituality and the means by which human beings can develop a closer relationship with the Divine. From this perspective, religious laws are not standards against which humans are judged by the Divine "taskmaster" but are invitations and advice by the Creator to the creature as to how they may attain their full potential. Viewing religious laws and commandments as spiritual instructions rather than the adoption of an attitude that unless people meet some minimum level of righteousness in their life God will condemn them to eternal damnation is more in harmony with the basic perception of Christian belief that God is love. Such a view does not make salvation any easier in the sense that there is less responsibility on the part of humankind; if a person does not follow the instructions and learn the lessons, they will not attain the knowledge, wisdom, and spiritual maturity that is, in fact, salvation. But viewing God as creator and developer rather than judge and jury can help people view life as a positive challenge rather than a negative test. This perspective is more in line with the approach to salvation espoused by the Eastern religions, showing, once again, that there can be more harmony between religious traditions than we often appreciate.

In both the Catholic and Protestant traditions the central factor in human salvation is the role of Jesus Christ. Both traditions hold that Jesus is the Son of God who came into the created world to effect the reconciliation of humankind to God. Both hold that this reconciliation was somehow accomplished by the crucifixion and resurrection of Jesus, although there are varying interpretations as to how these events accomplished this task. The view one takes depends on how one interprets the nature of the estrangement between the Divine and human. The orthodox view within both strains of Christianity is that Adam and Eve's disobedience in the Garden of Eden caused the separation of the

Sin and Salvation

human from the Divine for all of humanity. Whether understood mythically or literally, the blame rests with humanity. God was sinned against, and the result is human lost-ness or depravity, that is, human separation from God with no way for humans to atone for the sin and repair the breach. The problem seems to be God's intractability; even though humans caused the separation, God will not accept human repentance and atonement. To fix this problem, God had to send his own son into the human sphere to become the one human who was purely righteous and worthy of being in the presence of God. By allowing Jesus to suffer mortal death, although he did not deserve it, God was justified in raising him to immortal life to effect reconciliation of the human to the Divine. Jesus became the bridge between the human and divine spheres so that through him humans can claim a right to enter the presence of God. This is not an affirming view of God and has caused much dissension as church leaders have struggled with these implications. There is, however, another way to interpret God's program for humankind.

Central to Christian belief is the concept of resurrection. Christians affirm that although Jesus was killed by Roman crucifixion, he rose to new life, appeared in bodily form to many of his disciples, and eventually ascended into heaven after promising to return to the earth again at some undisclosed future time. Yet it is clear from the gospel narratives and interpretations by other writers of Christian scriptures that Jesus' post-resurrection body differed from his mortal body. The apostle Paul calls it a spiritual body and claims it to be the form in which all believers will one day be resurrected.[86] This spiritual body is held to be immortal and incorruptible, yet it had the appearance of Jesus' mortal body, even bearing the scars from his crucifixion wounds. In this body Jesus is said to have eaten food and was touched by some followers to confirm his reality, but he also appeared and disappeared in closed rooms.

What is described here is something of a paradox. The very term "spiritual body" seems a contradiction. While affirming the

---

[86] 1 Corinthians 15:42–57.

resurrection of the body, Christians also hold that God's essential being is entirely spiritual, and that those who are saved spend eternity in God's presence. While the reality of existence beyond this world is not well defined in Christian scriptures or tradition, some writers attempted to provide hints. The apostle Paul called it a mystery[87] and asserted that in this life we see into the nature of eternity dimly.[88] Keeping these limitations in mind, it is still useful to explore the idea of the after-life for what it can tell us about the nature of the Divine and the divine plan for humankind.

For the first disciples of Jesus, the promise of his return to earth was a major determinate in their actions and expectations. The Book of Acts records that some of the followers of Jesus sold their possessions, pooled their resources and joined together to worship, celebrated the Good News and essentially waited for Jesus to return and set all things right in this world. There is a sense in which this expectation was based on the Jewish belief in the coming of a Messiah. In fact, many early Christian seemed intent on convincing other Jews that Jesus *was* the promised Messiah. Although the belief in a Messiah was variously interpreted, Jewish prophets had foretold the coming of a divinely appointed and anointed leader who would assume the throne of David and lead the Jewish people to prominence, freedom, and everlasting prosperity. In Jewish tradition, this was to be the culmination of history and the fulfillment of human destiny. In some scenarios this triumph was to be accomplished by warfare between the forces of good and evil; in others it was to be a peaceful transformation, with the peoples of the world acknowledging the superiority of the Messiah's teaching and leadership. As time passed, the expected triumphal return of Jesus did not occur. Christian disciples continued to die normally and Christianity spread beyond Jewish culture. The disciple's understanding of Jesus changed from Jewish Messiah into the glorified Christ as universal Savior.

---

[87] 1 Corinthians 15:51.
[88] 1 Corinthians 13:12.

Sin and Salvation

The Jewish vision of the kingdom of God, while oriented to this world, also required a mysterious transformation of the natural world.

> "The wolf also shall dwell with the lamb, and the leopard shall lie down with the kid; and the calf and the young lion and the fatling together; and a little child shall lead them. And the cow and the bear shall feed; their young ones shall lie down together; and the lion shall eat straw like the ox. And the sucking child shall play on the hole of the asp, and the weaned child shall put his hand on the cockatrice' den. They shall not hurt nor destroy in all my holy mountain; for the earth shall be full of the knowledge of the Lord, as the waters cover the sea."[89]

This passage of course may be interpreted poetically or figuratively rather than literally. But the Jewish view of the fulfillment of the covenant between God and the Jewish people does tend to be understood as resulting in a physical society in which all people enjoy peace, prosperity, and the joy of family and friends. The natural evils of the present world are no longer a danger to people. Christianity adopted this vision of the kingdom of God but combined it with the more graphic and traumatic events foretold in Christian scriptures concerning the universal fate of humankind. In the Jewish and Christian traditions, the ultimate salvation of both individual human beings and humankind collectively is tied up with the end of human history and the created world as we know it.

In highly symbolic and mythical language, the New Testament book of Revelation foretells the coming end of human history through much turmoil and suffering to a triumphal but cataclysmic finale. In this accounting, the righteous are resurrected into a temporary earthly kingdom ruled by Jesus Christ for a thousand years. Presumably those involved will have spiritual

---

[89] Isaiah 11:6-9 IV.

bodies in the nature of Jesus after his resurrection. Then the unrighteous will be resurrected for one final period of trial and temptation, allowing them to choose between good and evil. Subsequently, the unrepentant unrighteous will be defeated and cast out by the judgment of God. This final judgment based on the choices made in human life, apparently including this period of resurrected life, determines who will remain in the presence of God or be cast into outer darkness or the lake of fire. Significantly, the material world is done away. The nature of the new heaven and earth that replaces it is unknown, but as it is the abode of God, it can be inferred to be a spiritual realm described as a city called the New Jerusalem. This harks back to the Jewish vision of the end of human history but includes both God and the Messiah having dominion over the eternal city.

But what is the state of the people at the end of human history and in the interim period between mortal death and resurrection? The information provided in scripture about existence beyond mortal life is both limited and highly symbolic. The Gospels provide little attributed to Jesus in this regard. Jesus does talk about the existence and importance of heaven, but does not describe it or define the nature of life within it. Some Jewish prophets and John the Revelator add more images, but these are highly symbolic. This is because once again they are trying to put into words insights beyond the common experience of humankind. We must approach this subject with caution and a sense of tentativeness to avoid reaching unwarranted conclusions and dogmatic statements. Yet prophets, seers, and mystics throughout the ages have tried to share the visions they were given, so there must be value for people in trying to understand something about the afterlife.

The Swedish mystic Emanuel Swedenborg (1688 – 1772) claimed to have had multiple visions of the eternal realms over a thirteen-year period. His books *Heaven and Hell*[90] and *Divine Love and Wisdom*[91] describe in some detail the nature of heaven and of hell and the condition and activity of those who inhabit

---

[90] West Chester, Pennsylvania: Swedenborg Foundation, 2003.
[91] Ibid.

them. He describes heaven as having three levels providing varying degrees of association to the Divine. Hell also has variations appropriate to the degrees of evil chosen by its inhabitants. Central to Swedenborg's understanding of the placement of souls in the afterlife is the principle that each is where they have chosen to be. By the exercise of their free will on earth, each person determines their closeness to the Divine both in mortal life and in eternity.

The American prophet Joseph Smith Jr. also left several messages concerning the afterlife. These writings follow the themes provided in the Biblical record but elaborate on and interpret them. Of primary interest with regard to the nature of the afterlife, Smith and a colleague, Sidney Rigdon, shared a vision in February 1832 which they afterward recorded.

> "Thus saith the Lord, concerning all those who know my power, and have been made partakers thereof, and suffered themselves, through the power of the Devil, to be overcome, and to deny the truth, and defy my power;
>
> they are they who are the sons of perdition, of whom I say it had been better for them never to have been born;
>
> for they are vessels of wrath, doomed to suffer the wrath of God, with the Devil and his angels, in eternity, concerning whom I have said there is no forgiveness in this world nor in the world to come;
>
> having denied the Holy Spirit, after having received it, and having denied the only begotten Son of the Father; having crucified him unto themselves, and put him to an open shame;
>
> these are they who shall go away into the lake of fire and brimstone, with the Devil and his angels, and the only ones on whom the second death shall have any power; yea, verily, the only ones who shall not be redeemed in the due time of the Lord, after the sufferings of his wrath;

for all the rest shall be brought forth by the resurrection of the dead, through the triumph and the glory of the Lamb, who was slain, who was in the bosom of the Father before the worlds were made.

And this is the gospel, the glad tidings which the voice out of the heavens bore record unto us, that he came into the world, even Jesus to be crucified for the world, and to bear the sins of the world, and to sanctify the world, and to cleanse it from all unrighteousness;

that through him all might be saved, whom the Father had put into his power, and made by him; who glorifies the Father, and saves all the works of his hands, except those sons of perdition, who deny the Son after the Father has revealed him;

wherefore he saves all except them; they shall go away into everlasting punishment, which is endless punishment, which is eternal punishment, to reign with the Devil and his angels in eternity, where their worm dieth not and the fire is not quenched, which is their torment, and the end thereof, neither the place thereof, nor their torment, no man knows;

neither was it revealed, neither is, neither will be revealed unto man, except to them who are made partakers thereof;

nevertheless, I, the Lord, show it by vision unto many; but straightway shut it up again; wherefore the end, the width, the height, the depth, and the misery thereof, they understand not, neither any man except them who are ordained unto this condemnation.

And we heard the voice saying, Write the vision, for lo, this is the end of the vision of the sufferings of the ungodly!

And again, we bear record for we saw and heard, and this is the testimony of the gospel of

Sin and Salvation

Christ, concerning them who come forth in the resurrection of the just;

They are they who receive the testimony of Jesus, and believed on his name, and were baptized after the manner of his burial, being buried in the water in his name, and this according to the commandment which he has given, that by keeping the commandments, they might be washed and cleansed from all their sins,

and receive the Holy Spirit by the laying on of the hands of him who is ordained and sealed unto this power;

and who overcome by faith, and are sealed by that Holy Spirit of promise, which the Father sheds forth upon all those who are just and true;

they are they who are the church of the Firstborn;

they are they into whose hands the Father has given all things:

they are they who are priests and kings, who have received of his fullness, and of his glory, and are priests of the Most High after the order of Melchisedec, which was after the order of Enoch, which was after the order of the only begotten Son:

wherefore, as it is written, they are gods, even the sons of God; wherefore all things are theirs, whether life or death, or things present, or things to come, all are theirs, and they are Christ's, and Christ is God's; and they shall overcome all things;

wherefore let no man glory in man, but rather let him glory in God, who shall subdue all enemies under his feet;

these shall dwell in the presence of God and his Christ for ever and ever:

these are they whom he shall bring with him, when he shall come in the clouds of heaven, to reign on the earth over his people;

these are they who shall have part in the first resurrection;

these are they who shall come forth in the resurrection of the just;

these are they who are come unto Mount Zion, and unto the city of the living God, the heavenly place, the holiest of all;

these are they who have come to an innumerable company of angels; to the general assembly and church of Enoch, and of the Firstborn;

these are they whose names are written in heaven, where God and Christ are the judge of all;

these are they who are just men made perfect through Jesus the mediator of the new covenant, who wrought out this perfect atonement through the shedding of his own blood;

these are they whose bodies are celestial, whose glory is that of the sun, even the glory of God the highest of all; whose glory the sun of the firmament is written of as being typical.

And again, we saw the terrestrial world, and, behold, and lo;

these are they who are of the terrestrial, whose glory differs from that of the church of the Firstborn, who have received the fullness of the Father, even as that of the moon differs from the sun of the firmament.

Behold, these are they who died without law; and also they who are the spirits of men kept in prison, whom the Son visited, and preached the gospel unto them, that they might be judged according to men in the flesh, who received not the testimony of Jesus in the flesh, but afterwards received it;

these are they who are honorable men of the earth, who were blinded by the craftiness of men;

these are they who received of his glory, but not of his fullness;

these are they who receive of the presence of the Son, but not of the fullness of the Father; wherefore they are bodies terrestrial, and not bodies celestial, and differ in glory as the moon differs from the sun;

these are they who are not valiant in the testimony of Jesus; wherefore they obtained not the crown over the kingdom of our God.

And now this is the end of the vision which we saw of the terrestrial, that the Lord commanded us to write while we were yet in the Spirit.

And again, we saw the glory of the telestial, which glory is that of the lesser, even as the glory of the stars differs from that of the glory of the moon in the firmament;

these are they who received not the gospel of Christ, neither the testimony of Jesus;

these are they who deny not the Holy Spirit;

these are they who are thrust down to hell;

these are they who shall not be redeemed from the Devil, until the last resurrection, until the Lord, even Christ the Lamb, shall have finished his work;

these are they who receive not of his fullness in the eternal world, but of the Holy Spirit through the ministration of the terrestrial; and the terrestrial through the ministration of the celestial; and also the telestial receive it of the administering of angels...who are appointed to be ministering spirits for them, for they shall be heirs of salvation.

And thus we saw in the heavenly vision, the glory of the telestial which surpasses all understanding; and no man knows it except him to whom God has revealed it."[92]

The vision of Smith and Rigdon quoted above needs to be approached with a good deal of caution for several reasons;

---

[92] Doctrine and Covenants 76:4-7.

Divine Providence: God's Plan for Humankind

1. All visions of spiritual things require interpretation and expression in words which may not be adequate for conveying the reality of what was experienced.

2. The prophets have only their own experiences and context from which to draw in interpreting visions. For Smith and Rigdon, the context was the beginning of a new religious movement which they hoped would put Christianity back on the right track. They approached all questions during this time from the point of view that God was entrusting them with the task of correcting errors, inadequacies, and heresies that had crept into Christian belief and practice.

3. The vision was given in the context of a prayerful inquiry about a scriptural passage from the Gospel of John concerning the resurrection of the good and the evil.[93] While their question was answered by the Spirit in the way of inspiration, the vision subsequently opened beyond their need or expectation at this time. Thus the experience transcended inspiration and went into revelation. While the two are closely related there is a different purpose for each. Inspiration, normally initiated by the human seeker struggling with concrete issues, is often specific and practical, clarifying and contextualizing the issue involved. Revelation tends to be new information initiated by the Divine in self-disclosure of the divine nature. For Rigdon, the vision was apparently a new experience and there is little evidence he contributed much to its interpretation. But Smith had experienced both inspiration and revelation before. While we can never know with certainty, and while we can never limit God's methods of revelation, there is strong indication that in the interpretation of this vision Smith was influenced by his focus on the question of the just and the unjust and by his preoccupation with organizing and justifying his fledgling movement. In short, there is indication that Smith tended to interpret this vision not as a prophet but as a priest.

A few months later, in December 1832, Smith sent a letter in which he again addressed the issues of resurrection and the after-

---

[93] John 5:29.

Sin and Salvation

life. The letter was sent to a colony of church members who had traveled to the United States western frontier to establish a community in which they hoped to exemplify the teaching of the church. Smith refers to the message as the "Olive leaf . . . the Lord's message of peace to us."[94] The language of this letter is poetic and inspirational and frames his understanding of the glories in less parochial and doctrinaire terms than the earlier interpretation quoted above.

> "Now, verily I say unto you, that through the redemption which is made for you, is brought to pass the resurrection from the dead. And the spirit and the body is the soul of man.
>
> And the resurrection from the dead is the redemption of the soul; and the redemption of the soul is through him who quickeneth all things, in whose bosom it is decreed, that the poor and the meek of the earth shall inherit it.
>
> Therefore, it must needs be sanctified from all unrighteousness, that it may be prepared for the celestial glory; for after it hath filled the measure of its creation, it shall be crowned with glory, even with the presence of God the Father;
>
> that bodies who are of the celestial kingdom may possess it for ever and ever; for, for this intent was it made and created; and for this intent are they sanctified.
>
> And they who are not sanctified through the law which I have given unto you, even the law of Christ, must inherit another kingdom, even that of a terrestrial kingdom, or that of a telestial kingdom.
>
> For he who is not able to abide the law of a celestial kingdom, cannot abide a celestial glory; and he who cannot abide the law of a terrestrial kingdom, cannot abide a terrestrial glory; he who cannot

---

[94] Doctrine and Covenants 85, preface.

abide the law of a telestial kingdom, cannot abide a telestial glory; therefore, he is not meet for a kingdom of glory.

Therefore, he must abide a kingdom which is not a kingdom of glory.

And again, verily I say unto you, The earth abideth the law of a celestial kingdom, for it filleth the measure of its creation, and transgresseth not the law.

Wherefore, it shall be sanctified; yea, notwithstanding it shall die, it shall be quickened again, and shall abide the power by which it is quickened, and the righteous shall inherit it:

for, notwithstanding they die, they also shall rise again a spiritual body, they who are of a celestial spirit shall receive the same body, which was a natural body: even ye shall receive your bodies, and your glory shall be that glory by which your bodies are quickened.

Ye who are quickened by a portion of the celestial glory, shall then receive of the same, even a fullness;

and they who are quickened by a portion of the terrestrial glory, shall then receive of the same, even a fullness;

and also they who are quickened by a portion of the telestial glory, shall then receive of the same, even a fullness;

and they who remain shall also be quickened; nevertheless, they shall return again to their own place, to enjoy that which they are willing to receive, because they were not willing to enjoy that which they might have received.

For what doth it profit a man if a gift is bestowed upon him, and he receive not the gift? Behold, he rejoices not in that which is given unto him, neither rejoices in him who is the giver of the gift."[95]

The treatment of the glories in the letter is a slight variation from that in the vision, but it upholds the basic structure for the afterlife. Keeping the above cautions in mind, the vision and letter can provide some insight into the nature of the divine plan for humankind with regard to the idea of salvation. The gospels do not record Jesus talking about the afterlife in specifics except for heaven and hell. His statement that in his Father's house are many mansions could be interpreted as such but is vague. It is the apostle Paul who in his first Corinthian letter mentions the three glories, likening them to the sun, moon, and stars. Smith's vision and the subsequent letter are an extensive elaboration of Paul's rather enigmatic reference. If we look for the principles that apply to all of humankind, we can see the following:

1. Damnation is not the default condition for humankind. Contrary to what some teach, salvation in the broad sense of being in relationship with the divine in eternity does not require compliance with some minimum number of laws or practices. Rather, damnation, eternal separation from the Divine, requires specific choices made with the full knowledge of what one is doing. Those who end up apart from the Divine have experienced the reality of the Divine and rejected it.

2. The idea that damnation is an option is the strongest assurance that human free will is real; the choices we make have real consequences, including the choice to deny our Creator.

3. The three glories described in the vision correspond to relationships with the three persons of the Triune God. Celestial glory is being in the presence of God the Father, or God in God's essential spiritual being. Celestial bodies are those like the glorified Christ. Those who enter this glory will come with Christ to reign on a transfigured earth for a thousand years. Terrestrial glory is being in the presence of God the Son, or God as concerned with the natural creation. This involves the Son not in

---

[95] Doctrine and Covenants 85:4-7.

his earthly body, but in his resurrected body. Those who enter this glory acknowledge Christ and worship him but do not have the spiritual maturity to be in the presence of God in God's essential being. Telestial glory is being in the presence of God the Holy Spirit, or God as the life force of the world. People experience this Spirit in various ways and to various degrees depending on what they are willing to receive and believe.

4. The glory a person experiences depends on the choices they have made in their life on earth or in the post-resurrection period of earthly existence mentioned above. In spite of the specific criteria Smith assigns, a more universal set of criterion is discernable. Celestial glory requires choices that place primary focus on spiritual values in life. Spiritual maturity is achieved by learning to see life with the eyes of God and to live with the attributes of God. The letter speaks of a resurrection of the earth itself as the abode of the celestial kingdom. We do not know what such a transfiguration might entail, but since it is to be the place where God in God's essential being dwells, it must be some type of spiritual existence. The transformation apparently takes place after the thousand-year reign of Christ and the final judgment. This interpretation underscores the spiritual nature of all creation. Nothing created by God is ever lost.

5. Terrestrial glory is the realm where God the Son rules. No description of it is given. Likewise, the nature of telestial glory is less defined but is an eternal existence in which God the Holy Spirit rules and angels minister to the inhabitants.

6. The vision and letter leave many unanswered questions. We are well advised to leave judgment as to who qualifies for each to God and trust his justice and mercy. From the human point of view, we are responsible for the choices we make in this life within the context in which these choices are made. The critical choices are whether and to what extent we are responsive to the Spirit of God. The criterion that Jesus consistently holds up is not our words or intentions, but how our actions demonstrate in what and whom we believe.

7. The exploration of the glories deals only with the end times and the eternal disposition of individual souls. It says

Sin and Salvation

nothing of the state of our spirits in the interval between mortal death and our resurrection, except that those who are deemed evil or unjust in this life spend the period in the prison house where they apparently receive instruction and exposure to a greater reality than they were willing to accept in life. The end of humankind requires a reuniting of body and spirit for full participation in eternal life.

Viewing sin and salvation not as compliance with some set of laws, but as relationship between the Divine and human, makes divine providence available and applicable to all people in all times and places. Religion then becomes the depository of hope, a bridge rather than a barrier for humankind. This does not mean that the consequences for doing evil in the world can be glossed over; all choices make an eternal imprint on the human soul which must be erased and overcome in order for an individual to improve their relationship with the Divine. The extent to which such corrections are possible is not for human beings to judge, but the degrees of relationship to the Divine outlined above imply eternal consequences for choices in this life.

Divine Providence

"Then [Taiowa], the infinite, conceived the finite. First he created Sotuknang to make it manifest, saying to him, 'I have created you, the first power and instrument as a person, to carry out my plan for life in endless space. I am your Uncle. You are my Nephew. Go now and layout these universes in proper order so they may work harmoniously with one another according to my plan.[96]*"*

—Hopi Myth

The nature and operation of divine providence is a part of every major religion but is expressed in different terms.[97] Hinduism and Buddhism tend to see the material world as *Lila*, divine play, in which all of the creatures are incidental. But because creation is spun out of the Divine, all creatures are also divine at their core. Each must find a way through the layers of *Maya*,

---

[96] Quoted in Novak, *The World's Wisdom*, 345-346.
[97] This chapter is focused on Christianity. The brief characterization of divine providence in the other major religions is not a criticism nor does it explore the rich diversity of thought within each. Rather, it is intended to lift up the commonality of the basic principle of free will at the heart of human response in the context of all religious faith.

Divine Providence

unreality that masquerades as reality, to uncover the Divine within. In this process we have no divine help,[98] but only the divine law of *Karma*, wholly consistent rules of cause and effect by which each *jiva*, or soul, may learn to discern reality from the superficial. The Hindu/Buddhist doctrine of transmigration of souls, or reincarnation, provides all the time in the world for each being to eventually discover that it is actually an undifferentiated part of the Divine. Buddhism has developed some pathways for the completion of the journey to *Nirvana* within one lifetime, sometimes with the help of a *Bodhisattva,* a spiritual helper or guide, but essentially it still discounts any divine help. Likewise, Hinduism provides guided pathways, and some individuals who have achieved success in discerning spiritual reality choose to provide support and advice for others. Progress toward the goal of freedom from the illusions of the material world depends on choices made by the individual.

Taoism holds that divine reality is neutral with regard to the individual, available for all to realize but providing no active help. All persons are part of the Tao, or ultimate reality, and are therefore immortal, but Taoism provides little explanation concerning the nature of existence beyond mortal life. Some persons who have developed spiritual awareness choose to help others along the way. From the human perspective, each individual is responsible for finding the truth of the Tao.

Confucianism developed a belief in the support of familial ancestors for those presently living in the mortal world. The ancestor's limited influence may be positive or negative, depending on the respect given them. In many respects, the divine realm is an extension of the mortal world, just grander in scope and bliss. It is presided over by the first ancestors of the Chinese people in hierarchical fashion. Confucianism says nothing about the non-Chinese world. It should be remembered that K'ung Fu-tzu never actually espoused a religion and that it was his follow-

---

[98] The Great Hindu Epics are stories of manifestations of the Divine interacting with and guiding humans along the way. While inspirational and instructive, these stories are considered mythical rather than historical and humankind can expect no intervention in support of their quest.

Divine Providence: God's Plan for Humankind

ers who developed religious interpretations and rituals based on the practical moral teaching they inherited. The Chinese religions assume the immortality of individual persons who pass on to an afterlife the nature of which is determined by the moral character and choices of the individual in this life.

Judaism was the first major religion to develop the concept of one Creator God for the entire world. This understanding was a gradual expansion of the tribal god idea and carries with it the covenantal relationship between God and the Jewish people. In this relationship, God promises to bless and protect the Jewish people and the people pledge to be faithful in serving God. Initially, the covenant idea defined serving God ritually and legalistically, but through the revelatory work of the Jewish prophets, the idea expanded to incorporate all that God was doing; the people were to be a blessing to all nations. God is active in history, seeking to guide and control the chosen people through blessing and punishment according to their faithfulness. God has spoken historically through the Jewish prophets to provide comfort, guidance, and chastisement as required. The destruction of the temple in Jerusalem in 70 C.E. and dispersion of the Jewish people throughout the Roman Empire and beyond effectively put an end to the ritualistic expression of the covenantal relationship between God and the Jewish people. Throughout the Common Era, God's guidance and control was provided through the scholarship and inspiration of the rabbis who interpreted the Torah and the collective wisdom of the Jewish leaders through the years. Ritual observance became more personal, but many Jews continue to look for the restoration of the Temple and the re-establishment of the throne of David. Judaism still believes that God is active in human history, although the decimation of the Jewish people in the Nazi Holocaust has made affirmation of the special relationship between God and the Jewish people virtually untenable for many modern Jews. On an individual basis, Jews espouse a wide range of belief concerning the afterlife, but most continue to believe that each person's choices and actions in this life determine the character and quality of that afterlife.

Divine Providence

Islam holds that all human activity is under the control of Allah who wields that control with mercy and justice. Human beings must simply learn to submit to whatever comes with gratitude and praise. Faithfulness to the practices of Islam assures each person eternal salvation, but not necessarily mortal prosperity and protection. Present-day Islam, while not unified in belief concerning other faiths, tends to hold that only those responsive to their beliefs and practices have a hope of reaching Paradise, usually pictured as an extension and enhancement of all the best of mortal life.

Christianity has struggled with the concept of divine providence. The central role of Jesus, believed to be God Incarnate, made divine providence personal, and the role of God the Holy Spirit, available to every individual, reinforced the idea. Yet Jesus' teaching concerning the kingdom of God made divine providence a corporate issue as well. Roman Catholicism has emphasized the role of the church leadership in receiving and interpreting the divine will for individuals. Protestantism has emphasized personal responsibility for receiving God's guidance from the Holy Spirit, most often through the Bible. When Christians have been oppressed, they have tended to rely on personal support from God, but when they have been in positions of power they have tended to claim divine support for their causes, armies, and economic and political systems. Like the Jews, many Christians have subscribed to the Piety/Prosperity theory; when a person or group is properly pious, God blesses them with protection and prosperity in this life. When adversity strikes, it is because of sinfulness.

The work for which the American prophet Joseph Smith Jr. is most widely known, the Book of Mormon, was published before he received and recorded his creation myth visions.[99] Included in the book is an account of God's plan for humankind in

---

[99] The Book of Mormon was first published in 1830 in Palmyra, New York. Over the years it has been republished many times, with a variety of editorial emendations, almost entirely of a grammatical, typographical nature. The original theological message has remained intact. .

the words of a sixth-century BCE prophet named Lehi. It provides in one condensed version (II Nephi 1:65-121) the essential outline of divine providence.

> "For the Spirit is the same, yesterday, to-day, and forever.
>
> And the way is prepared from the fall of man, and salvation is free.
>
> And men are instructed sufficiently, that they know good from evil.
>
> And the law is given unto men.
>
> And by the law, no flesh is justified, or, by the law, men are cut off.
>
> Yea, by the temporal law, they were cut off; and also by the spiritual law they perish from that which is good, and become miserable for ever.
>
> Wherefore, redemption cometh in and through the holy Messiah: for he is full of grace and truth.
>
> Behold, he offereth himself a sacrifice for sin, to answer the ends of the law, unto all those who have a broken heart and a contrite spirit; and unto none else can the ends of the law be answered.
>
> Wherefore, how great the importance to make these things known unto the inhabitants of the earth, that they may know that there is no flesh that can dwell in the presence of God, save it be through the merits, and mercy, and grace of the holy Messiah,
>
> Who layeth down his life according to the flesh, and taketh it again by the power of the Spirit,
>
> That he may bring to pass the resurrection of the dead, being the first that should rise.
>
> Wherefore, he is the first fruits unto God, inasmuch as he shall make intercession for all the children of men;
>
> And they that believe in him, shall be saved.
>
> And because of the intercession for all, all men come unto God;

Divine Providence

Wherefore, they stand in the presence of him, to be judged of him, according to the truth and holiness which is in him.

Wherefore, the ends of the law which the Holy One hath given, unto the inflicting of the punishment which is affixed, which punishment that is affixed is in opposition to that of the happiness which is affixed, to answer the ends of the atonement;

For it must needs be, that there is an opposition in all things.

If not so…righteousness could not be brought to pass; neither wickedness; neither holiness nor misery; neither good nor bad.

Wherefore, all things must needs be a compound in one;

Wherefore, if it should be one body, it must needs remain as dead, having no life, neither death nor corruption, nor incorruption, happiness nor misery, neither sense nor insensibility.

Wherefore, it must needs have been created for a thing of nought;

Wherefore, there would have been no purpose in the end of its creation.

Wherefore, this thing must needs destroy the wisdom of God, and his eternal purposes; and also, the power, and the mercy, and the justice of God.

And if ye shall say there is no law, ye shall also say there is no sin.

And if ye shall say there is no sin, ye shall also say there is no righteousness.

And if there be no righteousness, there be no happiness.

And if there be no righteousness nor happiness, there be no punishment nor misery.

And if these things are not, there is no God.

And if there is no God, we are not, neither the earth, for there could have been no creation of things, neither to act nor to be acted upon; wherefore, all things must have vanished away.

And now...I speak unto you these things, for your profit and learning:

For there is a God, and he hath created all things, both the heavens and the earth, and all things that in them is;

Both things to act, and things to be acted upon;

And to bring about his eternal purposes in the end of man, after he had created our first parents, and the beasts of the field and the fowls of the air, and in fine, all things which are created, it must needs be that there was an opposition;

Even the forbidden fruit in opposition to the tree of life; the one being sweet and the other bitter;

Wherefore, the Lord God gave unto man, that he should act for himself.

Wherefore, man could not act for himself, save it should be that he was enticed by the one or the other.

And I, Lehi, according to the things which I have read, must needs suppose that an angel of God, according to that which is written, had fallen from heaven;

Wherefore he became a devil, having sought that which was evil before God.

And because he had fallen from heaven, and had become miserable for ever, he sought also the misery of all mankind.

Wherefore, he said, unto Eve, yea, even that old serpent, who is the devil, who is the father of all lies; wherefore he said, Partake of the forbidden fruit, and ye shall not die, but ye shall be as God, knowing good and evil.

And after Adam and Eve had partaken of the forbidden fruit, they were driven out of the garden of Eden, to till the earth.

Divine Providence

And they have brought forth children; yea, even the family of all the earth.

And the days of the children of men were prolonged, according to the will of God, that they might repent while in the flesh;

Wherefore, their state became a state of probation, and their time was lengthened, according to the commandments which the Lord God gave unto the children of men.

For he gave commandment that all men must repent;

For he shewed unto all men that they were lost, because of the transgression of their parents.

And now, behold, if Adam had not transgressed, he would not have fallen; but he would have remained in the garden of Eden.

And all things which were created, must have remained in the same state which they were, after they were created; and they must have remained for ever, and had no end.

And they would have had no children; wherefore, they would have remained in a state of innocence, having no joy, for they knew no misery; doing no good, for they knew no sin.

But behold, all things have been done in the wisdom of him who knoweth all things.

Adam fell, that men might be; and men are, that they might have joy.

And the Messiah cometh in the fullness of time, that he may redeem the children of men from the fall.

And because that they are redeemed from the fall, they have become free for ever, knowing good from evil;

To act for themselves, and not to be acted upon, save it be by the punishment of the Lord, at the great and last day, according to the commandments which God hath given.

Wherefore, men are free according to the flesh; and all things are given them which are expedient unto man.

And they are free to choose liberty and eternal life, through the great mediation of all men, or to choose captivity and death, according to the captivity and power of the devil;

For he seeketh that all men might be miserable like unto himself."

For hundreds of years Christian churches have approached the subject of divine providence from the human perspective: "What must I do to gain God's favor so that I may be saved, blessed, protected, or made to prosper?" In its popular form, Christian believers seek to deal with the uncertainties and apparent hostility of the natural and social world by appealing to divinity to intervene in favor of ourselves and our group. Even in its more classical form it has tended to focus on the questions, "What does God's law require?", "How can I know God?" and "What must I do to obtain eternal life?"

Revelations make it possible for us to try to look at the issue of divine providence from God's point of view. From such a perspective, we see things differently. The creation myth explored earlier coupled with the above expression of divine providence indicates the following:

1. God created human beings as essentially spiritual beings, "in the image of God." The spiritual world is the ultimate reality of existence and the "abode" of God in God's essential being.

2. The natural world was created as a neutral venue for an essential developmental stage of humankind by providing separation from God's overwhelming presence and allowing us to exercise our free will. It is temporary and finite, in spite of its vastness and duration beyond human comprehension. It is comprehended by eternity, by God.

3. Life in this natural world is transitory, that is corruptible and mortal; all natural life ends.

4. This natural world and the temporary existence humans experience in it consist of both good and evil. From God's perspective, that which brings people closer to God is good and that which increases their separation from God is evil. Since God created human beings to be in relationship with the divine presence, this value system resonates with human beings as well.

5. Free will requires that the choices people make have real consequences, not only in the natural world but also for the eternal realm because such choices have spiritual content. Thus, the nature and degree of relationship people develop with God in this life determines their status when they return to the spiritual realm. What happens in the spiritual world is largely unknown, and probably unknowable, by humans.[100] The manner in which individuals exercise free will in the spiritual realm is beyond human understanding and not addressed directly by Christian scriptures, although there has been much speculation over the centuries.[101]

6. God provided from the foundation of the world for the possibility of reconciliation of human beings to God. This is the meaning of the incarnation of God the Son, his teaching, his miracles, or demonstration of the power of the spiritual over the material, and the commission to his disciples to carry on the

---

[100] The Swedish mystic Emanuel Swedenborg devoted the latter part of his life seeking to explain to humanity his understandings of the nature and function of the eternal realms based on multiple visions he claimed to have had. Mystics in all religious traditions have done likewise. Such writings can help people focus and contemplate on this subject, but still require each person to decide for themselves what to believe or how to understand the eternal world.

[101] For a discussion of this question in the Christian tradition, see Simon Francis Gaine, *Will there be Free Will in Heaven?* (London: T & T Clark, 2003). The treatment in this book covers the dominant ideas of Christian thinkers over the centuries. However, these views are based on assumptions as to what constitutes blessedness in the spiritual realm for which there is little evidence or support in scripture.

ministry of reconciliation of humans with God, to represent him to others.[102]

7. Evil is championed in this world by Satan, represented as a being who knowingly chose to defy God to try to become a power in his own right. Whether Satan is understood as an actual being or a mythical personification of opposition to God, the opposition is real and active in this world. All living things must struggle for survival; all living creatures act primarily from self-interest. Among humans, the opposition manifests itself not only in terms of survival, but also in terms of ego and the appetites that attract people to focus primarily on the material world in opposition to the spiritual. Both the natural and spiritual worlds are essentially good; they fulfill the purpose of their creation. It is the disproportionate focus by human beings on the natural world and personal gratification that perpetuates our separation from God and the divine realm

The further implications of trying to adopt the divine perspective include the following:

1. The morality of individual choice is not absolute from the human perspective; rather it depends on the possibilities and the influences impinging on the person at the time the choice is made. The natural world is complex, and each individual is born into it in a unique set of circumstances. Further, as a being develops from infancy to childhood to adulthood, they are subjected to the choices of other people, choices largely outside the individual's control. Thus, each choice a person makes is made in a specific and unique set of circumstances. The morality of the choices depends not on how it measures up to some set standard, some list of "dos and don'ts," but how it measures up against all the other options available to the person, given the influences at that time and place.

2. This statement of the human situation is often called situational ethics. If we consider only the inter-human aspects, the term applies. However, from the divine perspective, there is an absolute morality involved as well. We have too limited an un-

---

[102] II Corinthians 5:19–21.

derstanding of even ourselves to make such moral judgments. The absolute standard is not a human standard; rather, the absolute standard for moral choice is whether that choice moves one toward or away from God. The judgment of the morality of any choice is God's, not ours.

3. Such judgment does not require a pronouncement or intervention from God in each instance; rather, because the natural world is wholly derivative from and dependent on the spiritual world, morality is a function of the very nature of creation. In a sense, the Hindu concept of Karma is true. But the Divine can also affect the process in favor of an individual's spiritual development. This understanding treads a middle ground between the Eastern view of an uninvolved divine reality and the concept found in Islam and fundamental Christianity that all activity in the created world is caused by God.

4. The morality of human choice is inherent in the natural world, but human beings do not have the ability to comprehend all of the factors impinging on any given choice. Rather, the consequences of individual choices are played out in the realm of subsequent events. As humans develop their spiritual sensibilities they learn to feel their way toward God. God, however, also has free will and can affect mundane events within the self-imposed limitations which God has stipulated for the natural world. The governing criterion for this world is that God seeks to draw all people to him, but will not overwhelm human free will without the express consent of the person involved. But this does not mean that a person's choice to leave events in God's hands will ensure the person's desired outcome. God may deem it in the person's best interest to leave any action in the control of the person. Thus, God is both active and entirely constant with respect to the created world.

5. The exercise of moral choice requires people to consider the needs and benefits of other people or entities in the natural world as well as the individual doing the choosing. Every choice people make affects not only them but also others around them, and, in the final analysis, the situation of the natural/social world. In that world, all things are related and affected by all

other things. Science is increasingly confirming the radical interrelatedness of the natural world.

6. Sin may be defined as separation from God. Our state of sin is simply the distance we are from the divine presence. Acts of sin move us farther away from God while acts of repentance and reconciliation move us closer. Since the world in which we function is dynamic, even failure to act can result in our being moved closer or farther from the Divine. Thus, it is true that since the mythical creation and fall of Adam and Eve humans in this world are born in a state of sin. The difference in this version of the creation myth from that in the received text is that this is a state for which Adam and Eve were not morally responsible, nor are we morally responsible for being estranged from God by nature of our entrance into this state. God places us here as an essential phase in our creation as free and responsible beings. Each person is morally responsible for their own choices within the context that the choices are made. There is no guilt associated with our initial mortal condition, nor is God angry with us or with our first parents. God's attitude toward each of us is love.

7. The Son of God did not have to die to assuage God's wrath but simply to fulfill the nature of mortality to which we are all subject in this phase of our existence. God became incarnate to live for us and show us how to live in relationship to God. From God's point of view, the greatest sacrifice God made was to choose to limit his divinity by presenting to us a mortal persona; Jesus' primary sacrifice occurred at Christmas, not at Easter. Jesus' mortal death was necessary for him to become the first fruits of the resurrection process, which is the ordained fate of all humankind. But, by his mortal death he regained his true nature. The cruelty of his mortal death is not a measure of the debt owed to God, but rather a measure of the distance from God which the society in which he choose to live out his mortal life had moved. It was not atypical; such is the human condition that every age of human history has moral evils for humans to confront, abet, or ignore. This is the crucible in which human free will is forged and the measure of one's salvation determined.

8. We have no way of judging the development and testing of the free will of those persons who experience minimal mortal life. Infants who die within a few moments of birth, those born with severe limitations of their mental or physical capacities, and others who seem not to have the opportunity for making moral choices must be left in God's hands. There is reason to believe that all persons are born innocent, free from responsibility for their state of separation from the Divine. Only as free choice is exercised do we become responsible for our choices.

9. The Eastern doctrine of reincarnation appears attractive to some as a means by which all people could be given an equal chance at spiritual development. The revealed religions of the West do not provide for such a possibility. Rather, we have the active participation of the Divine throughout mortal life and must trust in the justice and mercy of God to handle the fate of all persons righteously.

Divine providence is God's program for the development of individual persons in the image of God, with free will and the right to choose the manner and extent of our relationship with God and other people. This is God's work and glory and the expression of divine love for his creation. The active operation of divine providence in the natural world is the work of God the Holy Spirit, the sustaining force for all natural life and the divine presence with which human beings may interact throughout their mortal life time. God is present to each person to the extent the person opens themselves for support and guidance.

For religions that assert divine neutrality or indifference to the human condition and the Law of *Karma*, the issue of why bad things happen to good people and the innocent suffer is explained by bad behavior in a previous incarnation. But for the religions that claim active divine control or involvement in human affairs this question causes concern. There is no simple answer: each situation is unique and the result of a combination of factors. However, there are some generalities that can be suggested.

The adversities of mortal life are the crucible of human moral/spiritual development; in confronting these, our qualities of compassion, fortitude, problem solving, and cooperation are developed. That there *is* adversity is basic to divine providence. Natural adversities, such as weather phenomena, competition among life forms, and the inevitable decline and decrepitude inherent in the cycle of life are common to all human beings and are morally neutral. But adversities created by human actions and choices, whether individual or societal, are the moral responsibility of those causing them. This does not make them any easier to bear, but it does provide arenas in which human development can occur. Here both our actions and our failures to act carry mortal and eternal consequences. The role of the Divine in this arena is to provide comfort and support to victims, guidance and strength to those trying to do the right thing, and forgiveness to those trying to change their behavior in positive ways.

In December 1830, while working on revisions to Genesis precipitated by his earlier revelations pertaining to the creation myth, Joseph Smith Jr. received another revelation.[103] This was an extensive elaboration of the story of Enoch, which in the received text is only a few verses.[104] This enigmatic reference states, "Enoch walked with God: and he was not; for God took him." The common interpretation of this passage is that Enoch was translated to heaven without dying because of his righteousness. In Smith's version Enoch responds to God's call to preach to the people to convince them to turn away from their unrighteousness. Enoch is assured of God's support and is granted a vision of the future outlining both the salvation of the righteous and the containment of the wicked. Enoch's ministry eventually results in the establishment of a group of righteous people who gather into a city. Because of the intransigence of the remainder of society, God takes Enoch and his entire city to heaven to preserve it until the last days.

> "And it came to pass, that the God of heaven looked upon the residue of the people, and wept;

---

[103] Recorded as Section 36 of the Doctrine and Covenants and also incorporated into Joseph Smith's revised version of the Bible as Genesis 7:1–78.
[104] Genesis 5:18–24 KJV.

and Enoch bore record of it, saying, How is it that the heavens weep, and shed forth their tears as the rain upon the mountains? And Enoch said unto the Lord, How is it that thou canst weep, seeing thou art holy, and from all eternity to all eternity?...

The Lord said unto Enoch, Behold these thy brethren, they are the workmanship of mine own hands, and I gave unto them their intelligence in the day that I created them.

And in the garden of Eden gave I unto man his agency; and unto thy brethren have I said, and also gave commandment, that they should love one another; and that they should choose me their Father.

But, behold, they are without affection, and they hate their own blood;...

And among all the workmanship of my hands there has not been so great wickedness as among thy brethren; but, behold, their sins shall be upon the heads of their fathers; Satan shall be their father, and misery shall be their doom; and the whole heavens shall weep over them."[105]

This revelation illuminates some of the principles of divine providence in relation to the role of the Divine:

1. It reaffirms the perspective of the new creation myth provided by Joseph Smith concerning the function of human agency in the development of humankind.

2. It reaffirms that the fundamental characteristic of the Divine is love and compassion.

3. It reaffirms the reality of the consequences of human choices for us as well as the positive or negative conditions these choices create for those who come after us.

4. It reaffirms the reality of adversity as a fundamental characteristic of mortal life. Satan, whether understood as a being or

---

[105] Genesis 6:35, 39-41, 43 IV.

the personification of opposition, is an active part of human experience.

5. It reaffirms that the Divine has provided the means by which people can choose to develop their relationship with divinity. In another section of the revelation the role of God the Son as redeemer of humankind is reiterated.

The function of divine providence in every aspect of human life bears witness to the full control and active involvement of the Divine in the development of human beings in the image of God, beings with full awareness and the hope of eternal bliss. From the human perspective, the challenges of life can seem more than anyone should have to bear. Yet when we become aware of the processes involved to make us fully human, we can only affirm the judgment of the Apostle Paul:

> "For as many as are led by the Spirit of God, they are the sons [and daughters] of God.
>
> For ye have not received the spirit of bondage again to fear; but ye have received the spirit of adoption; whereby we cry, Abba, Father.
>
> The Spirit itself beareth witness with our spirit, that we are the children of God;
>
> And if children, then heirs; heirs of God, and joint heirs with Christ; if so be that we suffer with him, that we may also be glorified together.
>
> For I reckon that the sufferings of this present time are not worthy to be named with the glory which shall be revealed in us.
>
> For the earnest expectation of the creature waiteth for the manifestation of the sons [and daughters] of God.
>
> For the creature was made subject to tribulation not willingly, but by reason of him who hath subjected it in hope;

Divine Providence

Because the creature itself also shall be delivered from the bondage of corruption into the glorious liberty of the children of God." [106]

---

[106] Romans 8:14-21 IV.

Meaning and Purpose in Mortal Life

*Unless we find some significance in our lives,
we mortal men and women fall very easily into despair.*[107]
—*Karen Armstrong*

If we understand divine providence to be God's plan for humankind, what should be the human response? From the human perspective the question still remains, "What does the Lord require of me?" Taking a more positive approach, the question is, "What can I do to align myself with God's purposes and possibilities for me?" Christians find themselves in a position similar to members of other faith traditions: one must seek to discern the reality of the created world, the divine perspective, and the possibilities available for participation in the divine program for this world and humankind. It is significant that all humankind is on an equal footing in our approach to divine providence at the practical level. Eastern religions rely on their scriptures, traditions, and the teaching of spiritual masters to help those who choose to become pilgrims on the way. Judaism has the law and the prophetic writings of scripture as well as a long tradition of

---

[107] Armstrong, *The Battle for God*, xv.

rabbinical scholarship to guide their people. Islam has the Qu'ran, the record of Mohammad's teachings, and the guidance of current and past scholars. Each tradition has schools of mysticism for those who seek direct experience of the Divine in this world. It is the theologians and mystics of each faith who illuminate the pathway and discern the parameters for finding meaning and purpose for those who follow that way. Christians also have scriptures, traditions, and spiritual masters, but in addition they testify that the active presence of the divine spirit is available to all who seek it and open themselves to it.

The luminaries of the great religions all present a vision of a spiritual reality superior in every sense to the existence of ordinary human life. They assert that the highest meaning of human life is to be found in aligning oneself with this reality, but they also maintain that in some measure this spiritual reality permeates and animates the created world. While humankind's ultimate task is to transcend this present finite existence, one is also able to participate to some degree in the higher reality while in this life. Meaning and purpose in human life is to be found in such participation. All religions that attribute personal traits to divinity identify the primary attitude of the Divine toward humankind as love, mercy, and compassion. Divinity is equally understood to be uncompromising toward actions and attitudes in humanity that ignore or defy the divine will whether knowingly or in ignorance. The balance of mercy and justice attributed to divinity is also reflected in the nature of the created world. Eastern religions emphasize that happiness and fulfillment in mortal life are attained by understanding and aligning ones attitudes and actions with the laws and nature of the created world, by seeking to harmonize oneself with the natural forces that permeate the world as we find it. Both Eastern and Western traditions agree that the Divine is the source of both happiness and misery; they simply differ as to whether the Divine acts intentionally by divine will or automatically by impersonal divine law.

The focus of a religion rests where its adherents most clearly see or sense the Divine. For primal religions and major traditions that grew out of them, such as Taoism and Shinto, the Divine is found primarily in the natural world. Followers of these religions or those whose culture was shaped by them give priority to the preservation and glorification of the natural world. Religions that grew out of social and political stresses, such as Judaism, Islam and Confucianism, place emphasis on social and political justice and the development of the resources of the natural world for the benefit of humanity. Religions that grew out of dissatisfaction with the efficacy of existing religious practice, such as Buddhism and Christianity, focus on doctrine and dogma and the practical utilization of the resources of the natural world to support the spread of their faith. Hinduism's judgment that the material world is not ultimately real has encouraged its adherents to view it with an air of practicality, to be used or ignored as suits the individual's stage of spiritual development.

These generalizations of the world's religions do not take into account the subsequent development of a more systematic treatment of humankind's relationship to the created world in each of them. But the foundational values continue to adhere. They illustrate how each tradition has different values which color for their followers their attitude toward the natural world, their view of persons following other faith traditions, and, most importantly, their sense of responsibility for their actions in this life. All religions pay attention to personal interaction, holding that how we treat each other reflects our core values and the nature of the ultimate reality expressed in the religion's foundational vision. All major faiths hold to standards of fairness, compassion, and mutual support, at the least with respect to those who share our perspective and, as the highest expression of our faith, extended to all humankind. All major religions struggle against the human tendency toward egoism and hold that higher purpose and meaning involves seeking the good of others.

Two modern trends have introduced complications not faced earlier that affect how humanity pursues meaning and purpose; these are the rise of science and technology and the rapid increase in population. Largely the product of Western Christian society, modern science and technology spawned the industrial revolution, which has since spread throughout the world. The benefits of technology in food production and distribution, health enhancement, and harnessing of energy have facilitated rapid growth in populations. Science and technology have expanded exponentially every individual's possibilities for engaging the material world. But paradoxically, the pressures of population have increasingly limited each person's ability to engage the natural world directly in a meaningful way. Science and technology have increased the amount of energy and material resources demanded by each person, and the increase in population has compounded these issues so that the total exploitation of natural resources is threatening to exhaust the earth's supplies. Pressures of population and technology are also negatively affecting the earth's biosphere and contributing to accelerated changes in weather patterns and reduced sustainability of food resources.

The increasingly complex organization necessary to exploit the world's wealth deemed necessary for the progress of civilization and judged beneficial for humankind reduces the number of persons having any elemental relationship with the natural world. This trend is most obvious in the increasing urbanization of the world's population. More people are dependent on the efforts of others for the basic necessities of life, and few of us have control of these necessities. The complexities of modern civilizations and the lag in moral and ethical development of science and technology have resulted in increasing disparity between those with control of resources and those with little or none.

As the natural world is a primary expression of the Divine for humankind, the increasing distance of modern people from direct involvement with the natural world reduces their exposure to and awareness of the Divine. Pre-modern people and those in less developed parts of the world today have had more direct dependence on the natural world for obtaining the necessities of life: food, shelter, and a sense of security. In the developed world, even the small percentage of the population involved with agriculture and the extraction of natural resources are in-

Divine Providence: God's Plan for Humankind

creasingly separated from nature through the imposition of machinery and other technologies between the person and the natural world. By its nature, technology is a means of dominance and control. Through it humankind manipulates the natural world for its own ends. Many scientists who study the natural world adopt a clinical attitude toward it which interferes with their perception of the Divine by which it came into being and by which it is sustained.[108] The increasing alienation of modern people from the natural world is a significant factor in their alienation from the Divine, the ground of meaning and purpose for each human being.

Although the Divine permeates the natural world, there is a closer connection between the human and the Divine. That is the spiritual essence within each living being. This essence is subtle and tends to masquerade as human consciousness. The difficult but rewarding disciplines of the mystics of the great religions is focused on helping disciples who seek the direct path to differentiate between that which is Divine and that which is human within the self, to suppress or control the self so that the Divine may become known. For those who respond to the pull of the Divine for reconciliation, the teachings of the great religions help discipline the egocentrism of the self and prioritize attitudes and actions. The two great commandments of Judaism and Christianity, to first love God and second love neighbor and self, are echoed in all the great faiths:

- He is the God in every way supreme! This is the sum of duty; do nothing to others which would cause pain if done to you. — Hinduism

- He who takes refuge with Buddha... is delivered from all pain. One should seek for others the happiness one desires for one's self. — Buddhism

---

[108] It is also true that a growing minority of natural scientists have an increasing appreciation for the unique and marvelous nature of our planet and the biodiversity it contains. More of them are sensing the presence of the Divine and recognizing the improbability of random chance and innate law explaining the material world. See Strobel, *The Case for A Creator,* for a popular, but informative example.

Meaning and Purpose in Mortal Life

- There is a Being wondrous and complete! Regard your neighbor's gain as your own gain, and your neighbor's loss as your loss. — Taoism

- Great, great is God, who ruleth man below! Do not unto others what you would not have them do unto you — Confucianism

- Your God is One God! There is no God but He! No one of you is a believer until he desires for his brother that which he desires for himself. — Islam

Christianity, more than the other great religions, focuses on love as the primary attitude and correspondence between the Divine and human. Other faiths hold the Divine in reverence and awe and counsel humility and obedience but do not project the same sense of intimacy and good will. Yet there is a sense of security in the path of obedience not found in some strains of Christianity. Christians who emphasize either ritual cleansing through authoritative ordinances, or those who rely solely on divine grace do find solace in their doctrinal stance. But those who emphasize works of righteousness and love as response to and evidence of grace struggle with the uncertainty of the adequacy of their performance. Yet this struggle is the essence of free will and the basis of divine providence.

The elegance of God's program for humankind is in its absolute universality. Every human life is of equal worth before God; every person's story is of equal importance in its eternal outcome. While the circumstances of each life differ and are largely determined by the choices made by ones ancestors, it is the choices each person makes for themselves that determines their standing with the Divine. Divine grace is expressed not in some blanket acceptance of a person's statement of faith but in the activity of the divine spirit constantly drawing the person toward the Divine and supporting each action the person takes in that direction. Such divine grace is balanced by divine judgment of actions that move a person away from the Divine. The primary venue for divine providence is the eternal realm, but its power and effect are also experienced in this world. By making choices that improve alignment with the Divine, one produces greater harmony in the natural world and increases the fulfillment of human potential. Sensing that one can affect the significance and value of one's life gives meaning and purpose in every circumstance.

The activity of the divine spirit in this world, while constant and totally faithful, is subtle and discernable only through the eyes of faith. The development of human free will requires a delicate balance between attraction toward and opposition to the Divine. That which opposes the Divine must exhibit a sense of meaning and purpose to be effective. The Hindu paradigm for human life recognizes this duality more overtly than the other faiths. The attractions of pleasure, worldly success, and civic duty all hold out promises of meaning and purpose. But Hinduism asserts that each of these ultimately fail in their promise and are proven to be finite. The Hindu doctrine of reincarnation allows each individual all the time they need to reach this conclusion independently. Faith traditions lacking this doctrine depend on the intervention of teachers in the form of scriptures, rituals, or spiritual guides to draw the distinctions between that which is eternally true and that which is deceptive in human experience. Yet whether confronted by life experience or by the assertions of religious traditions, each individual must decide what to base their live actions on.

Rather than basing it on how far one has traveled in their pilgrimage of reconciliation to the Divine, divine providence provides for judgment of eternal consequence on where one starts one's earthly journey, the opportunities one has, and the choices that move one toward or away from that goal. In this life, people may struggle to develop their relationship with the Divine, subtle and often hidden from view. But personal behavior relative to the created world, the degree of harmony with the natural world a person achieves provides a baseline of where one sees one's self in the scheme of things. Each person is also in relationship with other people, and the attitudes and actions one expresses in these relationships are reflective of the relative dominance of one's ego. Love for, and consideration of, others is a fundamental moral issue in every religion. Finally, a person's attitude toward, and participation in, the social, economic, and political life of one's community expresses their moral position and spiritual stature. This does not mean that what one achieves in life is the measure of their worth; rather, the integrity and intention of one's actions in the role they play in the human drama is the measure of one's standing with the Divine. In Jesus' words, "inasmuch as ye have done it unto one of the least of my brethren, ye have done it unto me."[109]

Meaning and purpose in modern life are found in taking responsibility for one's opportunities. For some, meaning and purpose may be limited to coping with personal needs and challenges—just getting through each day with a sense of dignity. Success may be measured in the small triumphs of survival and in showing love and kindness toward others. For those in a world consisting largely of family or village, meaning and purpose may be derived in demonstrating integrity in fulfilling one's role with good will and a positive attitude. For those with advantages of education and/or developed skills, meaning and purpose may be found in the furthering of a particular field of endeavor for the benefit of humankind. For those in positions of leadership, meaning and purpose may consist of faithfully mobilizing one's group to improve life's circumstances for all people, in inspiring others to enhance the lives of those less fortunate. For national and world leaders, meaning and purpose may be realized by working to improve security, prosperity, and justice for all civilization.

The opportunities one has carry with them the obligation to use those opportunities for the good of others, rather than as a means for controlling and oppressing for selfish ends. The miser, the tyrant, the bully, the leech, the lecherous, and the opportunist must all face the justice of divine providence. Our choices determine the essential character of our soul for good or ill. We are, in fact, our brother's and sister's and children's and neighbor's keepers to the extent that our actions affect their lives. Our sense of fulfillment of meaning and purpose in this

---

[109] Matthew 25:40 IV.

life is dependent on our contribution to the welfare of others, as this is reflective of the nature of the Divine which is innate within each of us. The divine nature is to create with the purpose of bringing into being others with immortal and eternal attributes, beings in the image of the Divine. Our highest purpose as creatures of the Divine is to assist in the realization of the divine purpose.

The Church

For God, who commanded the light to shine out of darkness, hath shined in our hearts, to give the light of the knowledge of the glory of God in the face of Jesus Christ. But we have this treasure in earthen vessels, that the excellency of the power may be of God, and not of us.
— II Corinthians 4:6–7 IV

God's plan for humankind functions whether we are aware of it or not, but it functions most effectively with those who comprehend and seek to apply it in their conscious thoughts and actions. To proactively develop our relationship with the Divine, we need to be cognizant of the existence of God, of our free will, and of God's intention for us. All major religions hold as a premise the existence of the Divine, whether as being deep within each person or as outside all persons. Each individual has an innate sense of the existence of some power greater than self. Whether this is sensed to be in the natural world or an unseen spiritual realm, its existence is felt as somehow related to each of us.

Some persons have a stronger awareness of the unseen power and put it into a framework for the rest of their society.

Divine Providence: God's Plan for Humankind

They become the contact persons between the seen and unseen worlds. Whether known as shamans, seers, prophets, holy men, priests, or by some other designation, they define the relationship between their people and the higher power the people sense. Over time, this relationship becomes formalized and systematized into a standard of traditional belief and practice. Often the pronouncements and teachings of the holy men and women are written down and become scripture for that society.

Holy men or women, particularly those who gain a reputation for having repeated access to the Divine, gather followers around them. These disciples seek to understand not only the message of the prophet but to also learn the secrets by which their access is enhanced. Each of the world's major religions developed initially around a single person or small group of people dedicated to the spiritual insights and apparent power of the vision they taught. Often it was the disciples of the primary prophet who first recorded and organized the teachings into a systematic exposition of the relationship between the human and Divine that became the religion. The disciples dedicated themselves to sharing a particular vision. Over time they organized into an identifiable group with structure, method of maintaining the purity of their vision, and further application of the vision to every aspect of human life. Their proximity to the visionary gave them authority to represent the teachings and practices of their leader. Whether known as priests, rabbis, imams, elders, or teachers, they became the leaders of the group known as a religious movement, or sect, or in the case of Christianity, a church.

Whether a particular movement promotes a new vision of the Divine within society or is a new interpretation of an existing religious tradition, the dynamics are similar. All major religions of the world have eventually developed a variety of branches with differing interpretations or emphases of the founding vision. Sometimes such branching is due to internal conflicts among religious leaders over doctrinal interpretation. Often these are presented as efforts to correct perceived misinterpretations, or heresies, of the original vision. Sometimes splits occur due to conflict of an administrative or political nature: who has the authority to control the organization. Sometimes divisions occur because of influences within secular society, such as the establishment of national churches or language usage. Occasionally, new branches within a religion occur in response to new visions given to individuals in a manner similar to those which initiated the original religion, causing a revised interpretation of an older vision.

Major world religions have both shaped and been shaped by the civilizations in which they arose. Most contemporary political states have held religion at arm's length both because they have had bad experiences with religions imposing unwelcome controls on the political and economic structures of society and because, increasingly, populations have included followers of a variety of religious faiths or none at all. The rise of science and humanism in Western society further loosened the hold of religion on people and the spread of Western influence through technology, military, economic, and political power has spread this trend worldwide. Some modern nations have attempted to integrate religious and political structures, most notably in the case of Islam in the Middle East. These efforts seem fraught with problems, but it is yet too soon to evaluate the full results of such developments.

Even when religion is kept separate from political control, it can permeate the society and exert enormous influence. Often, two parallel authoritative structures develop within society, one political and one religious, both of which determine the character and development of the people. This is particularly true when one homogenous religious movement dominates the society. Where multiple religious movements exist within one society, the influence of religion tends to be less pronounced and formative, yet it still provides moral and emotional focus for those citizens involved and helps shape the collective character of the society.

Unfortunately, in many instances, leadership within religions has created disaffection of people from belief in and dedication to the faith. Often such leaders have maneuvered to assert their authority over the laity by adopting a gnostic-flavored elitism (the secrets of the vision are only understood by those who have dedicated themselves to the ministry), over-simplification of the vision of the religion leading to ignorance of its spiritual truths, peer pressure (moral judgments on the behavior of sinners that cuts them off from the religion's blessings), and/or outright threat of eternal damnation (only the ordinances or rituals of the faith can assure acceptance by the Divine, and only the priest/shaman can perform the rituals properly). Such controlling behavior by religious leaders may be motivated by their desire to maintain the purity of the original vision or by their desire to assure the widest possible participation by the populace. However, the proper role of religious leaders is to serve as bridges between the Divine and human in accordance with the vision of the religion. This is done by teaching, guiding, nurturing, and testifying in word and deed of the tenets of the faith. As Jesus and other religious teachers have said, the most effective leader is the servant of all the people.

The rituals and ordinances can, likewise, be either positive or negative forces. These practices are intended to symbolize important spiritual truths; they are intended to involve the followers of the religion in acts of devotion; they are meant to allow worshipers to more fully participate with body and soul in the expression of their beliefs. But sometimes these rituals become substitutes for personal involvement, vicarious acts of devotion for which the meaning is no longer clear to the individual. Particularly where rituals are performed by the priests with the laity watching or responding by rote, the practices tend to lose their efficacy. Rituals performed in this manner tend to take on the character of appeasing or even coercing the Divine to accede to human wishes. Religion practiced in this manner tends to become a process of complying with a set of arbitrary divine laws to satisfy the minimum standards for acceptance.

When a religion becomes controlled only by priests or interpreters of the vision, it tends to calcify and lose its ability to bring the human and Divine into alignment. Religion requires prophetic infusions from time to time to refresh and re-animate its vision. Living, vital religions require an ongoing dialogue between the human and Divine, with the conversation able to be initiated by either party. When priests control, it is often difficult for prophets to get a hearing within the formal structure of the organization. This conflict between established organization and the visions of those who sense a need for renewal within it can lead to schism and the eventual splintering of the faith. This does not mean that the vision of every dissident is divinely inspired; heresy is a real danger for all belief systems. Dissidence may arise from a variety of motives: simple grabs for power and control to myopia or loss of vision to demonic interference in the progress of the faith movement. But if the leadership loses its humility and openness to new input from the Divine, fracture is almost sure to result. The Divine will proceed with its program by every means available and will not be thwarted by human weakness or willfulness. Prophets speak truly at the impress of the Divine; priests function rightly at the sufferance of the Divine.

A prophet is called to that function by the Divine; one cannot aspire to this calling or qualify for it by their own effort. Priests, on the other hand, are those who respond to the prophetic vision, devote themselves to following it, and qualify for ministry by study, devoted service, and openness to the confirming approval of the Divine. Prophets respond to the Divine; the Divine responds to the priest's call for divine support. Neither of these functions is innate within the individual but occurs as an ongoing and continually renewing commitment. A prophet does not become such as a right, nor is the function necessarily permanently attached to the individual. Rather, a prophet speaks for the Divine whenever the Divine decides to speak and the person decides to receive and transmit the message. A priest functions legitimately to the extent they seek and receive the inspiration or confirmation from the Divine to interpret and convey the meaning of the divine vision. Both function effectively when they faithfully serve as bridges between the Divine and human, when their ministry brings people into a closer relationship with the Divine.

Divine Providence: God's Plan for Humankind

A church, then, is a voluntary organization of people dedicated to developing their relationship with the Divine and committed to helping other people do likewise according to the church's vision. In Christianity, denominations function differently depending on both their vision and on the traditions developed over time. All churches have some organizational structure in which people function as authorities both for the organization itself and for the teaching and spiritual guidance of the members. In many denominations, leaders receive formal training and are supported by the general membership to carry out the functions of the church. In others, all members share in the responsibilities and ministries, each contributing what they can to further the programs and functions of the church. Some groups are primarily focused on the spiritual development of their own members, while others focus on outreach. Many have a combination of internal development and outreach. The effectiveness of any particular church in helping people develop a relationship with the Divine is determined by the collective choices of those making up the organization and the quality of the vision around which the organization is established.

In all religions there is a hierarchy of relative closeness between the human and the Divine.

1. First is the revelation on which the religion is based. This is the disclosure initiated by the Divine.

2. Second is the interpretation of that revelation by the prophets receiving the revelation. They always struggle to express in terms meaningful to their culture the transcendent experience of the Divine. This oral or written interpretation often becomes the primary scripture of the religion.

3. Third is the interpretation of the scripture and teachings of the prophet by disciples who attempt to preserve and apply the essence of the revelation and its significance to the lives of believers. Such interpretation becomes the doctrine, theology, and ritual of the religion. Often these interpretive writings become additional scripture and the disciples become the priests of the religion.

The Church

4. Fourth is the organization developed by the disciples to practice and disseminate the understandings of the prophets and priests throughout the culture in which the religion arises. In modern times, religious organizations often attempt to share their vision with all humankind.

5. Fifth are the programs produced by the organization to facilitate the practices and teaching. These include printed materials, broadcast media, and sub-organizations such as schools, classes, study, social and service groups. They also include procedures to finance the organization's activities.

Christian churches have generally been the human face of religion in Western society. Their reason for existence is to help people develop their relationship with the Divine. Yet many struggle against adopting societal standards of evaluating the effectiveness of their mission. In the eyes of those outside the organization their strength is often judged on numbers and financial assets. The temptation within the organization is to adopt these criteria as their own measure of success. Although many churches seem to be focused on the fourth and fifth levels, the true measure of success for a church is its faithfulness to its initiating vision, its effectiveness in interpreting and applying its vision to contemporary society, and its ability to share its vision with people throughout society. If the vision is powerful and relevant, these measures will bring people into relationship with the Divine. The splintering of Christianity into many denominations is evidence of the failure of church leadership to focus on the primary criteria over the centuries.

Nearly all Christian denominations see themselves as heirs to the original disciples of Jesus. They derive their authority either from unbroken descent from those disciples, as claimed by the Roman Catholic and Eastern Orthodox churches, or from inspired interpretation of the Bible, as claimed by Protestants. A few claim a new and unique revelation from the Divine and derive their authority from it. But all who claim Jesus Christ as their Lord seek to represent him and embody his teachings in contemporary society. The two great challenges of Christian discipleship are to evangelize the world and to establish the kingdom of God on earth.

Christianity has a long history of evangelism, of proactively sharing its beliefs with non-Christians to convert them to the faith. Churches have been the primary organizers and supporters of evangelism. This emphasis is the outgrowth of what Christians believe was the last commandment given to the disciples by Jesus prior to his ascension into heaven. Known as the Great Commission, this commandment is recorded in two variations in the Gospels of Matthew and Mark.

> "Go ye therefore, and teach all nations, baptizing them in the name of the Father, and of the Son, and of the Holy Ghost; Teaching them to observe all things whatsoever I have commanded you; and, lo, I am with you always, unto the end of the world."[110]

> "Go ye into all the world, and preach the gospel to every creature. He that believeth and is baptized, shall be saved; but he that believeth not, shall be damned."[111]

Through the centuries this commission has been understood in two different ways: as invitation or as mandate. Those who read these scriptures as mandate view Christianity as the church militant. This is the idea that only baptized Christians are saved; therefore Christianity must be adopted by all people for their own good. Christians are justified in using almost any means necessary to convert people. This approach emphasizes humankind's lost-ness and the divine requirement for compliance to the church's rule to merit acceptance by God. This legalistic interpretation of Christianity has contributed to many abuses, including colonization and subjugation of indigenous peoples, the Inquisition, the doctrine of predestination, and Manifest Destiny.

---

[110] Matthew 28:18-19 IV.
[111] Mark 16:14-15 IV.

The Church

Modern evangelical Christian denominations tend to be rooted in this interpretation of the Great Commission.

Those who interpret the Great Commission as invitation to Christ emphasize the creative and loving nature of God and Christianity as the church triumphant. While avoiding some of the abuses of the church militant, the church triumphant has often exhibited the self-centered smugness of those who believe themselves to be "in a good place." They have a secure relationship with their creator and sustainer. They view evangelism as openness to any who are attracted to Christianity, an invitation to all to come into the fold and join in the worship, study, fellowship, and occasional service provided by the church. The view of the church triumphant is that God will cause whatever needs to happen for the salvation of humankind in his own time and way. The job of Christians is to witness and celebrate the mighty acts of God in personal and corporate life and to respond generously and courageously whenever confronted with issues that are disruptive to the onward progress of human development and well-being. In modern times, the Roman Catholic and mainline Protestant churches tend to approach their religious practice in this manner.

Another grand theme runs through Christianity and impacts the nature of its churches. That is the concept of the kingdom of God. The record of the public ministry of Jesus in the gospels is replete with references to the kingdom of God. In the Jewish context in which that ministry was lived, the concept referred both to the hopes of the people for freedom from Roman rule and the re-establishment of the Jewish nation, and the apocalyptical culmination of human history in the fulfillment of the divine covenant. The highly symbolic New Testament book of Revelation reinforces the mythical imagery of the Old Testament book of Daniel concerning a cataclysmic finale to human history. But Revelation makes the reappearance of the glorified Christ the event that precipitates the end of the world. Jesus' resurrection, ascension, and promise to return created the context for the development of Christianity as a separate religion.

Yet Jesus' teachings include other concepts of the kingdom of God. One of these is the idea of a heavenly realm, the eternal abode of God the Father, the angelic hosts, and the resting place for the souls of all the righteous. Jesus prayed to his Father in heaven, and assured the Roman governor at his trial that his kingdom was not of this world. Shortly before his death, Jesus assured his disciples that he was going to his Father's mansions and would prepare a place for them there. But Jesus also taught his disciples to pray that God's kingdom would come on earth as it was in heaven, and he talked about love, compassion, and justice within society. From the human perspective, these two ideas are often in conflict and Christian churches have struggled through the centuries with them.

In the early years of Christianity, the disciples of Jesus were a persecuted minority who focused on the heavenly kingdom and the promised return of Jesus from that realm to defeat their persecutors and transform society. Martyrdom in defense of the faith was viewed as the highest witness of devotion. But when Christianity was adopted by the Roman Empire as the state religion, the church began to see itself as the embodiment of the kingdom of God on earth. With the blessing of the state, the church began to collect to itself the trappings and rituals of an earthly kingdom. While always presenting itself as the mediator between the people and the heavenly kingdom, the church asserted itself as the sole repository of divine approval and authority.

Even as the church worked to build its influence and control, some within its ranks rejected its worldliness and drew apart into simplicity and non-involvement to pursue the spiritual life. These dissidents sought to connect directly and personally with the Divine and to exemplify what they understood to be the true expression of the kingdom of God on earth. The contrasting views of the kingdom of God have been a significant factor pulling Christianity into its widely divergent communities of believers. Some denominations focus on helping their members cope with mortal life by drawing on the guidance and spiritual support of the Divine. These groups hold that the kingdom of God is within each individual. Others help their members prepare themselves for residence in the heavenly realm. These groups see the kingdom as beyond the mortal realm. Still others seek to precipitate the return of the heavenly kingdom to earth. Often called millennialists, they tend to draw apart from society in hopes of perfecting themselves to the point where God will either translate them to himself or descend to be with them, transforming the mortal realm into the eternal. Christianity remains divided over the nature of the kingdom of God, and whether religious belief and practice are intended to help individuals develop their relationship with the Divine or to help develop society and culture into an ideal state. If the life and teachings of Jesus are to be embraced by those who claim to be his disciples, both aspects must be recognized as true and be part of God's plan for humankind.

The church must be seen as supplemental to the primary working of God the Holy Spirit among all humankind. Reconciliation between the Divine and human is not, in the end, dependent on the church's work of evangelization nor its efforts to transform society into the kingdom of God on earth. Rather, divine providence works with each individual human being in the context of their earthly life. Each person's story is a sacred story in which their spirit interacts with the spirit of God to the extent the person allows. The church provides a framework to help people develop their own spirituality within the context of interpersonal relationships that characterize mortal life. It can provide intellectual, social, and emotional support for spiritual development. To the extent it is true to its founding vision and conveys the spiritual essence of that vision effectively, the church provides a benefit to humankind. But to the extent that it distracts people from a focus on the spiritual to a focus on its own survival and glorification as a human entity, the church becomes a barrier to spiritual development. That the Divine inspires men and women to engage in its efforts to mediate divine providence is a great gift of Grace to those responding to this calling.

From Believer to Disciple

Henceforth I call you not servants; for the servant knoweth not what his lord doeth; but I have called you friends; for all things that I have heard from my Father I have made known to you.
—John 15:15 IV

Judaism developed the concept of the covenant and the idea of a covenant people. While Judaism was being formed it was common for each ethnic group or nation in the Middle East to identify with a particular group of gods and to think of a mutual and exclusive loyalty between their group and their gods. National gods were identified with homelands and the prosperity of the group. When the group prospered and enjoyed control of their territory, the gods were honored and worshipped. When hard times came and there was defeat in battle and subjugation or displacement from the homeland, the old gods were abandoned and allegiance was transferred to new and more powerful gods.

    The Jewish people under the tutelage of their prophets took this concept to a higher level. Although they struggled as a nation to remain faithful, slipping often into the worship of the Canaanite gods and being chastised by their prophets, the Jews eventually realized that their God was not concerned just with them but was in fact the one and only God, the creator of the entire world and all people. Their relationship was not for the benefit of the Jewish people in opposition to all others, but was to be the means by which all the nations of the earth were to be blessed.[112] Time and again they tended to forget the larger nature of their covenant relationship to focus on their insecurity, their mistreatment at the hands of others, and their lack of glory in the eyes of other nations. Just as often their prophets called them back into the essence of their covenant. Often their insistence that they had a special relationship with God put them at odds with other faiths and made them a target for persecution, because the nature of that relationship was misunderstood both within and outside their community.

Judaism was not and is not a proselytizing religion; its followers do not see their mission as convincing other people to become a part of their covenant and their group. Rather, they see their responsibility as being keepers of the covenant and an example to other peoples of how to be faithful and righteous. The Jewish approach to dealing with the conflicting values and interests of the world's people is illustrated in a recent book by Jonathan Sacks, the Chief Rabbi of the United Hebrew Congregations of the Commonwealth. In direct response to Samuel P. Huntington's definitive analysis of the current world situation, *The Clash of Civilizations and the Remaking of World Order*,[113] Sacks' book, *The Dignity of Difference, How to Avoid the Clash of Civilizations*,[114] does not call for everyone to adopt a common faith, social paradigm, or philosophical perspective, but using concepts out of Judaism, he calls for tolerance, respect for each religion and social system, and honoring the inherent worth and dignity of each person on the planet. Huntington's analysis seems to make global conflict inevitable; Sacks' suggestions offer a way of taking the fear and animosity out of the relationships between differing systems, traditions, religions, and aspira-

---

[112] See Jonathan Sacks, *To Heal A Fractured World* (New York: Schocken Books, 2005), for a current expression of this concept within Judaism.
[113] Published by New York: Simon & Schuster, 1996.
[114] Published by London: Continuum, 2002.

tions. Huntington assumes a zero-sum game; Sacks affirms that there is enough and to spare if everyone is willing to share and trust in the generosity of divine providence and the human spirit. Huntington ends his book with a warning and a sense of hope based on mutual fear that the consequences of global conflict are too horrible to be countenanced, the Cold War mentality of the twentieth century. Sacks ends his book by calling for a *covenant* of hope, a voluntary commitment by all people to hold the worth of human dignity above self interest. This is traditional Judaism at its best. While it is idealistic in that it provides no program by which to convince people to adopt its perspective, it does reaffirm the fundamental premise that each of us bears responsibility for making the right choices.

Christianity began as an attempt by the prophet and teacher Jesus of Nazareth to recall the Jewish nation to its true purpose. The gospel accounts of the deeds and words of Jesus are filled with his flouting of Pharisaic restrictions and his denunciation of their legalistic interpretation of the Law and the Covenant. He tried to call the leadership and the people back into the essential focus of the covenant, being the example to the world of God's loving relationship with all of his creation. Jesus acted in the tradition of prophetic confrontation with the priestly, sectarian control of society. The story indicates that after being rebuffed by the Jewish leadership, Jesus reluctantly commissioned his followers to go their own way based on his teaching and the spiritual power with which he endowed them.

For some time, the followers of Jesus tried to continue his work of teaching, healing, and lifting up of the downtrodden and marginalized of society. They went to the synagogues and to the temple in Jerusalem to share their story and their mission but were also rebuffed by the Jewish leadership. The main stumbling block for the Jewish leadership was the claim by the followers of Jesus that he was

1. The Messiah,
2. Resurrected and glorified,
3. Coming again soon to usher in the New Age.

From Believer to Disciple

Initially, Jesus was acknowledged by many, including some in the Jewish leadership, to be a prophet and a healer. But when he used his power only for the sake of the sick and marginalized and not to promote the interests of the Jewish people against the Roman overlords, and would not even protect himself and his followers, they could not accept him as the Messiah. They would not see that any such use of divine power for partisan purposes was anathema to the covenant.

The concepts of resurrection and glorification were largely foreign to Jewish thinking. The Jewish idea of the kingdom of God was firmly rooted in this world.[115] Although they had some vague notion that the final triumph of the rule of God would involve miraculous transformation of the physical world, they were unprepared for the kind of personal triumph claimed for Jesus by his followers. Judaism at that point seems to have been so immersed in group identification that personal salvation was not given serious credence.

Although the Jews looked for deliverance in the form of a divinely empowered Messiah, they apparently were not able to see such a figure in the defeated and shamed Jesus who had succumbed to Roman control. The expectation of Jesus' imminent physical return proved to be unfounded and his followers were also forced to modify their thinking in this matter. But this was after the sect had been ousted from the Jewish fold and had embarked upon its own course as a separate religion.

In assessing the life and ministry of Jesus, those who became his disciples struggled to expand their thinking from the Jewish context in which Jesus had lived to apply it to all humankind. The Apostle Paul is credited with being a primary leader in this development. In doing so they adapted many Jewish themes, rituals, and concepts to a Christian perspective. One of these was the idea of the covenant. Christians proclaimed a new covenant with God. In doing so, they focused on the rejection of Jesus by the Jewish

---

[115] For a concise statement of the Jewish understanding of and outlook toward life, see "The Fundamental Outlook of Hebraic Religion in Will Herberg, *Judaism and Modern Man* (New York: Farrar, Straus & Giroux, Inc., 1951).

leadership of his day. One of the tragic consequences of this effort was the assumption they made that there could be only one covenant people; they assumed that God's covenant was withdrawn from the Jews and granted to the emerging Christians. Such an assumption was understandable in the light of two issues:

    1. The centuries-old belief of the Jews that they had been *uniquely* chosen by God to be his people, and

    2. The Christians' emerging belief that God himself had come to his people and had been rejected by them.

Once again, a concept which seems perfectly natural and logical from the human perspective is not necessarily so when viewed from the divine perspective. Is not God able to enter into covenant with whomever he wishes? Why does a covenant with one people preclude another covenant with another people? If the divine purpose is to bring all people into relationship with God's self, how can any of us presume that our relationship to God is exclusive? Do God's relationships with others lessen the meaning, purpose, and value of our relationship with him? The testimony of the world's peoples in all places and all times is that they are being called into relationship with the Divine. Insisting on special treatment from God is the essence of egoistic expression and the antithesis of divine grace and justice. At some level, every religion claims itself to be a unique expression of God's revelation or inspiration. Why does this seem to many to preclude God's revelation and inspiration to others?[116]

---

[116] In an interesting but somewhat enigmatic exchange recorded in the Gospel of John (21:21-24, English Standard Version), Jesus seems to address this question on a personal level. "When Peter saw him (John), he said to Jesus, 'Lord, what about this man?' Jesus said to him, 'If it is my will that he remain until I come, what is that to you? Follow me.' The saying spread abroad among the brethren that this disciple was not to die; yet Jesus did not say to him that he was not to die, but, 'If it is my will that he remain until I come, what is that to you?'" Joseph Smith inquired about this issue and recorded what he considered inspired clarification confirming the idea that John was to remain alive on earth until Jesus return. (See Doctrine and Covenants 7.) The issue for Jesus was not primarily John's unusual status, but the uniqueness of each person's choice and the idea that each person receives what they choose (within the divine plan) rather than some generic treatment.

From Believer to Disciple

What does it mean to be in covenant with God?

- Acknowledging God as the creator, the foundation of all existence.

- Acknowledging that God wills to be in relationship with humankind.

- Holding as the highest and best good for humankind conformity to the will of God.

- Being true to the particular vision that God has chosen to give to you, either directly or to those with whom you find the Spirit of God resonating.

- Being committed to a program of activity intended to further the work of God the Holy Spirit to reconcile all creation, particularly humankind, to God.

It will be useful here to draw attention once again to a theological/metaphysical concept that is both pervasive and largely unappreciated by most of us. This is the concept of the transcendence of God in God's essential being. All major religions teach the transcendence of God, that God is utterly other than the natural world in which we humans currently find ourselves. Though some Eastern religions hold that the natural world is ultimately unreal and only the divine transcendence is finally real, and the Western religions hold that the created world is fully real but finite and temporary, all agree that the Transcendent Divine is both eternal and utter unity. This means that this divine reality encompasses all that exists and that all things will ultimately come to the same realization, not just intellectually but actually.[117] However, while holding this fundamental theological/metaphysical concept, each religion also teaches that within the natural world the Divine is somehow manifest in some limited and partial way that allows humans to encounter it. The religions differ precisely on the issue of how the Divine is manifest to humankind.

The Swiss theologian Frithjof Schuon spent his life studying the world's great religions and wrote books exploring each of them. Though he is better known in Europe, he was an inspiration for similar exploration by American theologian and teacher Hous-

---

[117] "Thou believest there is one God; thou doest well; the devils also believe, and tremble."—James 2:19 KJV.

Divine Providence: God's Plan for Humankind

ton Smith. In 1984 Schuon published a book titled *The Transcendent Unity of Religions*.[118] The book includes an introduction by Smith in which the essence of Schuon's thesis is put into a diagram that I have found most helpful.[119]

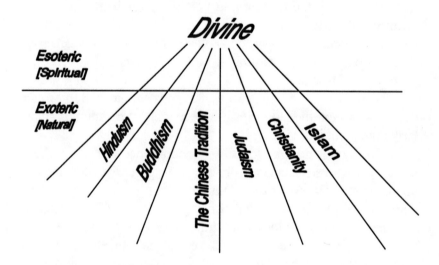

The diagram illustrates several significant concepts:

- The Divine, in the Divine's essential nature is One. Persons in the exoteric world view the Divine through the lens of their tradition which provides them with a manifestation of the Divine.

- Each of the world's major faith traditions has the *potential* of bringing persons into a full experience of the Divine.

- The line between the exoteric and esoteric realms is not impervious. Rather the natural world is permeated with and sustained by spirit. Likewise, there is a natural aspect to the spiritual realm in terms of forms and types. However, in the exoteric realm, the spiritual is subtle or hidden while in the esoteric realm the forms are eternal and incorruptible.

---

[118] Wheaton, Illinois: The Theosophical Publishing House.
[119] Ibid., xii.

- In the natural or exoteric world the individual traditions differ and the manifestation(s) of the divine characteristic of each tradition differ, and both are mutually exclusive from those of all other traditions. While they may have common characteristics, their essential manifestation is culture specific and possibly time specific and is not wholly transferable to other cultures. Time-specific issues are updateable within each tradition but require an appreciation of the internal historical developments within the culture and a clear understanding as to what is myth and what is history.
- Appreciation of the esoteric aspect of each religion requires a particular focus and discipline; apparently some persons in each tradition— often called mystics—are more inclined by their nature to pursue these. Moreover, the Divine is able to, and apparently does on occasion choose to disclose itself and its program to humankind.
- In the Hindu and Buddhist traditions each individual person must attain the Divine Presence through as many reincarnations in the exoteric world as it takes. In the revealed religions, God determines the final attainment of each person based on both the person's choices in one mortal lifetime and on divine justice and grace. Attainment of the Divine Presence in this life is rare and is not a requirement for the granting of salvation.
- A person will get closer to the Divine by moving vertically within a particular tradition than by moving horizontally between traditions. While we may appreciate the values of the different traditions, few people have the ability to really develop spiritually outside of their culturally-oriented nature. On the other hand, people who find that their traditional religion is a stumbling block rather than a bridge may be able to find a clearer path in another tradition. But once a path is chosen, spiritual development requires faith in and dedication to the way of that religion.
- The diagram does not deal with differences within the main religions, which are often more divisive than those between the great traditions. Nor does it provide a place for the so-called primitive religions of many indigenous peoples, nor the various

humanistic philosophies that substitute for religion for some people. This is because all such specific religions and philosophies have identity only within the exoteric region and that which defines them must be transcended to move into the esoteric realm. That is not to say that primitive religions are not spiritually based; in fact, many are more spiritual than the world religions in their exoteric forms. But primitive religions tend to base the spiritual in this world rather than see it as primarily transcendent. This is not a value judgment of these beliefs, but simply recognition of their nature.[120]

While appreciation of the value and potential of each of the world's great religious traditions provides us with a paradigm for universal hope for humankind, and affirms the view of each tradition that there is one Divinity responsible for all the created world, the differences between the traditions on the exoteric plane require that we acknowledge these differences in the choices we make. Each of us is born into this world in the midst of an exoteric belief system. Our view of divine providence is initially formed by the particular faith tradition of those who nurture us. Moreover, in order for us to believe that our religious faith holds out hope for our reconciliation to the Divine, we must affirm that the vision of the Divine that is the focus of our faith in the exoteric world is a true manifestation of Divinity in its essence, and that this vision can serve as a bridge to that which is ultimately real for humankind.[121] But believing this does not remove the conflict between our vision of the Divine and that of true believers in other faith traditions. They also believe their vision represents ultimate truth about the Divine. Only in the esoteric or spiritual realm is this conflict resolvable, and few of

---

[120] My characterization of the various religious traditions is not intended as a value judgment of any of them and certainly does not attempt in any way to explore the myriad differences within these traditions. They are, rather, based on published explorations of these faiths and are intended only to illustrate the broad differences in perspective, focus and understanding each provides.

[121] Again, "People have a profound need to believe that the truth they perceive is rooted in the unchanging depths of the universe; for were it not, could the truth be really important?" Smith, *Forgotten Truth*, v.

us are sufficiently involved in that realm to perceive the resolution. Moreover, those who do so perceive are seldom able to express it in terms acceptable to the majority involved with another particular religion.[122]

In addition to asserting that the Divine, in its essential nature, is the same for all religions, we must also assert that the divine plan for humankind is essentially the same as well.[123] Within the revealed religions the concept is clear; each individual is reconciled to the Divine to the degree justified by the choices they make in the context of their life and the essential teachings of their faith. God is able to judge righteously in this regard. Thus, whether Jew, Christian, or Muslim, those who respond to the spiritual teaching of their tradition with full intent and purpose are found acceptable. Having asserted this, what of those who choose evil, seemingly with sincere belief, as a result of nurturing by evil persons? It is certainly in the realm of possibility that individuals are effectively precluded from choosing freely because of being nurtured by people who have chosen to deny the Divine. In such cases, there is reason to believe that the responsibility lies with the nurturer and the victim of such nurturing is accorded mercy and forgiveness.[124]

But how can the workings of divine providence be understood in the Eastern traditions? How does the Hindu and Buddhist belief in reincarnation affect the attitude of followers of these faiths? If one believes that each person will eventually attain reconciliation to the Divine, does it matter how that person acts in this particular life cycle? Buddhism focuses a person on the negatives of life, the suffering and decrepitude each of us faces. In this it encourages proactive efforts to overcome these

---

[122] *"Those who say do not know, those who know do not say" Tao Te Ching*, Chapter 56.

[123] "In the same order of ideas, the following words of Saint Augustine may be cited: 'That which today is called the Christian religion existed among the Ancients and has never ceased to exist from the origin of the human race until the time when Christ Himself came and men began to call Christian the true religion which already existed beforehand' (*Retract.* I.13.3)." Schuon, *The Transcendent Unity of Religions*, 129.

[124] Numbers 14:11–20 IV.

Divine Providence: God's Plan for Humankind

conditions by positive behaviors individually and socially. But Hinduism takes a more relaxed approach, tolerating many materially-focused behaviors in the belief that each person must discover for themselves the emptiness and futility of following such a path. Once a person decides to pursue spiritual development, the pathways taught by Hinduism are positive, moral, and self-disciplining. Again, one must trust to divine wisdom, justice, and mercy to make the fate of each person a legitimate expression of their choices.

This raises the question of proselytizing. All the major world's religions, with the exception of Judaism, have had followers who felt it was their duty to share their faith and its blessings with other people and to encourage others to adopt their particular belief system. Judaism has always held itself to be the possession of one people, a particular line of descendants of the patriarchs Abraham, Isaac, and Jacob. Although they believe that as a people they are called to be a means of blessing all the other nations of the earth, they do not proactively encourage others to become Jews. Confucianism has also tended to remain a Chinese cultural phenomenon due to its roots in the ancient Chinese classics and its ancestor veneration. But in its early days, the disciples of Kung Fu-tzu aggressively spread the word within their culture and increasingly identified its teachings with the innate natural order of the world. Each of the major religions arose within a homogeneous culture, but as they grew, they inevitably pushed again other cultures and other faiths.

Both Christianity and Islam, however, believe they are specifically commissioned to take their faith to all people, and many within these traditions hold that there is no salvation for individuals outside their faith. Both of these religions have actively worked through much of their respective histories to proselytize as a sacred duty to their God and to their fellow humans. To the discredit of both faiths, some followers have actively forced conversion and submission to these faiths, militarily or through economic and political pressure. Fundamentalists in both these religions even today believe that conversion to their true belief is essential for salvation, and therefore, almost any means is justified to save people from the eternal disaster that awaits all who do not join them. Moderates in both these faiths, while rejecting coercion in any form, still hold that it is their duty to God and humanity to share their beliefs and invite others to join them.

It is necessary to differentiate between the conditions during the rise of each of the great world faiths and those of today. Each of the world's major religions arose and matured within a largely homogeneous cultural setting. Hinduism and Buddhism arose in the Indian subcontinent, characterized by an agrarian economy and a hierarchical political and social system in which each person knew from birth what was expected of them. When Buddhism later spread to other parts of Asia, it encountered similar cultures and found ready conditions for its adoption. Its focus on the personal as opposed to the social and political allowed it to mesh with Confucianism in China and later with Shinto in Japan without posing a challenge to either of those nationalistic religions. Confucianism and Taoism developed in China in much similar circumstances. Confucianism initially was more of a social and political ethic and only gradually began to explore the hierarchical, spiritual connection to family ancestors, going back to the First Ancestor, who took on aspects of a Creator-God. Even today, most Confucianists look to Taoism and/or Buddhism for deeper spiritual values and perspective. Judaism arose in the Middle East in turbulent and conflicted times. But it shared with its competitors a common set of principles: security, prosperity, and dominance for the nation relative to other nations were a reflection of the power and truth of the group's god and religion. Judaism later changed from being tied to place to being tied to the people by heredity, but always with the hope and promise of a return to the place it grew up. Christianity's milieu was the Roman Empire with its Hellenistic intellectual standards, Roman rule of law, and multicultural tolerance. But as an outgrowth of Judaism, it held to the idea of a covenant people responsible for the demonstration of the divine purpose for all of humankind. Yet it is a later interpretation that enlarged the commission to "go into all the world" from the then-understood world of the Roman Empire to the whole of humankind.[125] This is not to suggest that the later interpretation is inappropriate but to point out the context in which the initial commission was made and understood. Islam developed within Arab culture but with an awareness of both Judaism and Christianity with which it rubbed elbows in the world of commerce. In its early rapid expansion Islam was respectful and tolerant of both Judaism and Christianity and only later developed its forced conversion stance. The confrontations between Muslims and Christians that were most tragically played out in the Crusades were as much about political and economic power as they were about religion, and the religious motivations that were present were the product of theological developments in both religions that insisted on exclusive access to divine truth and salvation. Antipathy between Muslims and Jews is a much more recent phenomenon and also has much to do with control of territory and economic competition.

The rise of modern technology has changed the nature of society fundamentally from that which prevailed when the great world religions arose. The development of oceangoing ships began the great mixing of peoples and civilizations. Prior to that, the Jews had dispersed, often against their will, among other civilizations while retaining their own identity. The Jewish propensity to remain a separate people caused little concern within societies who tolerated these peculiar and sometimes useful people with no real challenge to their own culture and traditions. Chinese people also migrated widely, tending to retain their own identity and culture. But as transportation and communication

---

[125] "Certain passages from the New Testament indicate that for the Christian religion the 'world' is identified with the Roman Empire, which represented the providential sphere of expansion and life for Christian civilization. Thus, St. Luke wrote–or rather the Holy Ghost made St. Luke write–that 'in those days there went out a decree from Caesar Augustus that all the world should be taxed'…to which Dante made an allusion in his treatise on the monarchy when he spoke of the 'census of the human race'…Elsewhere in the same treatise we find the following: 'By these words we may clearly understand that universal jurisdiction over the world belonged to the Romans,' and also: 'I therefore affirm that the Roman people… has acquired… dominion over all mortals." Schuon, *The Transcendent Unity of Religions*, 22.

improved and economic development spurred the exploration for, and exploitation of, the world's resources, peoples holding different religious views became increasing intermingled. Those who traveled the most were Europeans bearing Christianity and Arabs bearing Islam. These two faiths, both with proselytizing mandates, spurred religious confrontation.

From the fifteenth century to the present day, the European powers and their New World descendants, dominated the flow of goods, peoples, and ideas around the globe. In the last century the great leaps in transportation and communication have transformed the cultural landscape even more radically and now the flow of peoples and ideas, including religious ideas, is in all directions and involves more diverse populations. Samuel P. Huntington's *Clash of Civilizations and the Remaking of World Order* is increasingly coming into focus.

So, what does it mean to be a Christian disciple in today's world? How is God's program, divine providence, being played out? The essence of divine providence remains the same: to encourage people to develop their relationship with God, to become reconciled to God which results in the realization of human potential. For Christians the words of the Apostle Paul sum up Christian faith and discipleship:

> "From now on, therefore, we regard no one from a human point of view; even though we once knew Christ from a human point of view, we know him no longer in that way. So if anyone is in Christ, there is a new creation: everything old has passed away; see, everything has become new! All this is from God who reconciled us to himself through Christ, and has given us the ministry of reconciliation; that is, in Christ God was reconciling the world to himself, not counting their trespasses against them, and entrusting the message of reconciliation to us. So we are ambassadors for Christ, since God is making his appeal through us; we entreat you on behalf of Christ, be reconciled to God. For our sake he made him to

be sin who knew no sin, so that in him we might become the righteousness of God."[126]

The last sentence of this passage can be confusing. J. B. Phillips translated it as, "For God caused Christ, who himself knew nothing of sin, actually to be sin for our sakes, so that in Christ we might be made good with the goodness of God." This concept is even clearer when we understand sin to be separation from God. The sentence then means that God the Father (the Divine in the divine essence) caused God the Son (the manifestation of the Divine in terms of the created world) who is fully at one with God the Father to become incarnate (a part of the created world separate from the eternal realm) so that people in the created world might have access to the divine realm, might be able to sense the reality of the divine life that is possible for each of us and the means by which we might attain that life.

It is significant that God's action described here says nothing about Jesus serving as a substitute blood sacrifice for Adam's and Eve's bad choice in the Garden of Eden. Christ accomplished the work of reconciling humankind to God by becoming human and living in harmony with the divine will. He certainly suffered an unjust and painful death, which showed his true humanity, but it was his life as a human being that makes possible our hope of becoming reconciled to the Divine. His resurrection and transfiguration back into his spiritual body demonstrated the realization of the hope that each of us have of eternal life by choosing to follow the pathway Jesus demonstrated in his earthly life and ministry. By inviting God the Holy Spirit to enlighten and empower our individual spirits we are able to live in this world in increasing harmony with the divine plan; we are on the way to becoming reconciled to God, to be made good with the goodness of God.

Christian discipleship, in the end, is a matter of choice, a matter of believing enough to live according to the perspective espoused by the Christian faith. This is equally true of disciples of any religious faith. Whether a religion is true depends on

---

[126] 2 Corinthians 5:16-21 NRSV

whether the religion leads people to become reconciled to the Divine. We have said that each of the world's major religions has demonstrated that it has that potential. But it is equally true that not every interpretation that divides the major religions into sects and denominations leads to that result. This is as true of Christianity as any of the others. It is also true that any one program for bringing people into relationship with God is not equally effective for all people. This is the case for several reasons.

- People are simply different: they have different personalities, different gifts and talents, different way of learning, and different life circumstances.

- Even within the same society, people are at different stages of their lives and cannot deal with the same information with equal effectiveness.

- People have different levels of interest and commitment because of their own free will.

Hinduism is more open than other religions in recognizing and trying to deal with differences in personality types. It has developed in its teachings four major paths to human/divine reconciliation which are worthy of consideration by people of other faiths.[127]

1. The Path of Knowledge – This path appeals to people with a reflective, reasoning bent. While not purely intellectual, it provides scope for people who live largely in their heads. Here God is perceived as infinite, undifferentiated Being and the goal is to become one with this Being.

2. The Path of Love – This path recognizes that feelings are basic to personality and that the greatest and strongest feeling that fosters a sense of joy is love. This path is the one most compatible with Christianity's central teaching that God is love, and that one's primary responsibility is to love God and to love other people in this world. Love requires relationship which means differentiation or personification of God.

---

[127] This information is derived from Smith, *The World's Religions*.

3. The Path of Work – This path appeals to people who find the greatest meaning in life by doing. This is a path of compassionate work, of seeking to deal with the ills of this life by solving the problems life throws at us. For those who follow this path the second commandment is their primary guide and the evidence of their commitment to the first. They agree with the poet Kahlil Gibran that "Work is love made visible."[128] Those who take this path see God as the rewarder of those who do good, who seek justice, who love mercy.

4. The Path of Experience – This path is taken by those we in the West call mystics. These are people who through personal spiritual disciplines seek to experience the Divine directly. Their goal is to retreat from the created world in order to see it with the eye of God and comprehend it with the mind of God. For these people God is Ultimate Reality and the result of following this path successfully is participation in this reality.

These four pathways have a long tradition within Hinduism and elaborate programs for each have been developed to guide pilgrims along their chosen path. The categories identified are neither exclusive nor comprehensive. Hinduism recognizes that each individual has a unique combination of characteristics and must develop their own path toward the Divine. Recognizing one's dominant nature puts a person into a program that moves them more naturally along the way. More importantly, the religion does not rate people or imply that one path is more spiritual or a higher way. All lead to the same goal and taking the path most compatible with one's created nature is fulfilling the divine intention if one can so state in the context of Hinduism's non-personal conception of the Divine.

While we in the West recognize the differing traits of people, Christianity has not done a good job of providing programs of ministry that take such characteristics into account. Within the secular world, modern society has developed a wide range of tools to help people discover their inherent giftedness. Whether it is the eneagram, Meyer-Briggs, colors or numbers, or spiritual

---

[128] Kahlil Gibran, *The Prophet* (London: Heinemann, 1926), 35.

giftedness, sociologists and psychologists have attempted to categorize differences in personal abilities and perspectives. In one sense, the splintering of Christianity into many denominations and sects is a tacit recognition of this reality, but such splintering seldom occurs gracefully and with good will. Rather, both sides of a split within a church tend to feel the other has gone hopelessly astray and must repent or be lost forever. The priestly strain within religions tends to latch on to a particular point of view and assume it to be the best, if not only legitimate, pathway to the transcendent God.

This does not imply that every conceivable approach to God is legitimate and able to bring people into relationship with the Divine. Many such paths have proven to be tragically barren and to lead to no good end. False religions driven by unscrupulous or pedantic people and demonic forces abroad in the world spring up like weeds in every society. Priest and prophet alike are charged with the responsibility of discerning spiritual values and guiding pilgrims in productive spiritual paths. Finally, each pilgrim is personally responsible for their own progress based on efforts expended, choices made, and grace and enlightenment received.

In the present world the Christian church and its members are called to embody and witness of the divine plan for humankind. This is what the mission of the church has always been, but the church has not always had a clear idea of the nature of the divine plan, nor the kind of witness needed. To restate ideas expressed in an earlier chapter, there are levels of focus in this process, and it is essential that the church understand which level it is holding up as primary:

- The first level is the reconciliation of individual human beings to God. This is the reason for the plan; this is the reason for the incarnation of God the Son; this is the final step in the process of the creation of humankind: it is bringing to pass the immortality and eternal life of human beings.[129] This is the divine

---

[129] Doctrine and Covenants 22:23b.

focus and humankind knows of it only because God chose to reveal it through the prophetic process.

- The second level is the divine plan, divine providence. Divine providence is the process by which persons may be reconciled to God. It is the continuous work of God from the beginning of creation; it is effected by the self-disclosure of God, centrally by the incarnation of God the Son, but continuously by the working of God the Holy Spirit through prophetic and inspirational intervention in human affairs throughout human history; it is the work of spiritual development by individual persons through prayer and meditation, service and study, work and worship. This is the primary level of human involvement with the Divine and must be the church's primary focus.

- The third level is the recruitment of willing human beings to assist others in developing awareness of divine providence. This is effected by the development of inter-human testimony of the Divine and the divine plan through scripture, religion, and "the foolishness of preaching."[130]

- The fourth level is the maintenance of the religion. This is effected by building the organization, providing opportunities, materials and places for worship, prayer, study, witness and service. It also involves the development of theology and the application of human talents and abilities in service programs of ministry.

In light of the above, what is the good news—the gospel—to which Christianity is called to witness?

1. God is actively working to create each person in the divine image; our prospects for a glorious future are bright even though we do not comprehend at this time all that entails. This is the basis of Christian hope.

2. Our relationship to God is largely up to us. God is doing everything possible to be available to us without overpowering or usurping our free agency. Our choices in this life determine our response to the divine initiative. This does not mean that the way is always clear and the choices easy or unambiguous. It is

---

[130] 1 Corinthians 1:21, and Romans 10:14, 15 IV.

the process of choosing and bearing responsibility for our choices that develops us in the image of God. There are real temptations trying to influence our choices away from God. These influences come from our own egos, from other people, and from whatever demonic forces are abroad in this world. But the divine essence in each of us is able to withstand such negative influences and control our destiny with the support of the Divine. This is the basis of Christian faith.

3. Our status with God is not a function of where we start out in this life, but of the direction we are facing relative to God and the direction our choices are moving us. In this sense, those of us born into privilege may be in greater risk of falling short than those born into adversity; God's criterion is the same for all, but the privileged have a tendency to feel they have already arrived and may not act as responsibly as those who know their life is a struggle.[131] Every person faces unique challenges and how these are handled either helps us grow spiritually or retards such growth.

4. When we choose to align ourselves to God and with God's plan for humankind, we may be invited by God into a covenant relationship. A covenant relationship is more than a personal agreement between God and the individual; it is not primarily about what I can do for God and what God can do for me. A covenant relationship is about becoming part of God's program for humankind, about working God's plan among and on behalf of humanity, about being God's ambassador in the world. It may be true that not all are offered the choice to enter into covenant relationship with God, but those to whom this choice is offered are accountable for their response.

5. A fundamental responsibility of those in covenant with God is to discern the divine intention for the current situation and the nature of the ministry needed to provide people with opportunities for developing their personal relationship with God.

---

[131] Hence, "It is easier for a camel to go through the eye of a needle, than for a rich man to enter the kingdom of God."—Matthew 19:24 IV. And, "For unto whomsoever much is given, of him shall much be required."—Luke 12:57 IV.

Divine Providence: God's Plan for Humankind

In this discernment, we are called to put aside our tendency to judge others in terms of our particular circumstances, and work with people where they are. It is not necessary that all people adopt our approach to the Divine, yet we must remain true to our faith and the pathway set before us.

6. As Christians we can only live authentically within the Christian tradition. But because we accept that all people are God's creation and all authentic revelations of the Divine are contextual in terms of culture and tradition, we can accept that there is more than one legitimate pathway to reconciliation between human beings and God. Moreover, when we acknowledge that the unity of religions only occurs at the esoteric level, our efforts are directed toward helping people move upward within their tradition rather than laterally from one tradition to another. This is not to say that we hide our witness or dilute the discipline of our faith. Rather, our witness becomes focused on living our faith overtly and testifying to the spiritual reality underlying the world. We testify to the love of God for all people by treating all people as God's beloved.

Within Christianity today, those who would become a covenant people will embrace the diversity of society while remaining true to their heritage and the spiritual vision that empowers it. By their discipline, they will marshal their resources on behalf of God's program for humankind. They will actively seek to discern this program and their stewardship responsibility for implementing it. While inviting all to participate in their mission, they will respect and encourage those of other faith communities to be true to the essential spiritual nature of their vision and mission.

Believing in God may assure our individual salvation, ensuring we will have an eternal relationship with the Divine. But discipleship involves actively working God's plan for all humankind. It is in discipleship that we can come closest to fulfilling our created purpose of being in the image of God. Salvation may be an achievable state, but discipleship is an ever-unfolding journey.

LaVergne, TN USA
17 December 2009
167378LV00002B/12/P